Working Together

Succeeding in a Multicultural Organization

Third Edition

George F. Simons, D.Min.

A Fifty-Minute™ *Series Book*

Menlo Park, California

1-800-442-7477

CrispLearning.com

Working Together

Succeeding in a Multicultural Organization

Third Edition

George F. Simons, D.Min.

CREDITS:
Senior Editor: **Debbie Woodbury**
Assistant Editor: **Genevieve Del Rosario**
Production Manager: **Judy Petry**
Design: **Nicole Phillips**
Production Artist: **Zach Hooker**
Cartoonist: **Ralph Mapson**
Illustrators: **Rich Lehl, Zach Hooker**

© 1989, 1994, 2002 Crisp Publications, Inc.
Printed in the United States of America by Von Hoffmann Graphics, Inc.

CrispLearning.com

02 03 04 05   10 9 8 7 6 5 4 3 2 1

Library of Congress Catalog Card Number 2002103376
Simons, George F.
Working Together
ISBN 1-56052-670-X

Learning Objectives For:

WORKING TOGETHER

The objectives for *Working Together, Third Edition* are listed below. They have been developed to guide you, the reader, to the core issues covered in this book.

THE OBJECTIVES OF THIS BOOK ARE:

❑ 1) To help you explore your thoughts, feelings, and attitudes about people different from yourself

❑ 2) To explain techniques for improving how you communicate and use language in a diverse setting

❑ 3) To increase your awareness of how you behave and interact with diverse colleagues and customers

ASSESSING YOUR PROGRESS

In addition to the learning objectives, Crisp Learning has developed an **assessment** that covers the fundamental information presented in this book. A 25-item, multiple-choice and true-false questionnaire allows the reader to evaluate his or her comprehension of the subject matter. To learn how to obtain a copy of this assessment, please call **1-800-442-7477** and ask to speak with a Customer Service Representative.

Assessments should not be used in any employee selection process.

About the Author

George Simons, M.A., D.Min. is founder and president of George Simons International, a global virtual consulting and training network. He is the creator and general editor of the award-winning DIVERSOPHY® training instruments and the www.diversophy.com Web site which offers intercultural expertise online.

With over 30 years experience in cross-cultural communication and global management, he is an internationally known counselor and author. Working in English, German, Spanish, Dutch, and French, he has served organizations both large and small in over 35 countries, recently among them Alcoa, Alstom, Nokia, Shell, Siemens, Teva, and Unilever.

In addition to *Working Together* and *Men and Women: Partners at Work* in the Crisp Fifty-Minute™ series, Dr. Simons has written, edited and co-authored numerous books, videos, and instruments in the field of diversity and intercultural management, most recently a book on *EuroDiversity* and a training manual on *Global Competence*.

His current activities include consulting, training, and keynote presentations on intercultural effectiveness and virtual teamwork. He is part of Management Centre Europe's regular faculty and serves on their online training initiative team. He is a member of the Editorial Advisory board of the *European Business Review*.

How to Use This Book

This *Fifty-Minute™ Series Book* is a unique, user-friendly product. As you read through the material, you will quickly experience the interactive nature of the book. There are numerous exercises, real-world case studies, and examples that invite your opinion, as well as checklists, tips, and concise summaries that reinforce your understanding of the concepts presented.

A Crisp Learning *Fifty-Minute™ Book* can be used in a variety of ways. Individual self-study is one of the most common. However, many organizations use *Fifty-Minute* books for pre-study before a classroom training session. Other organizations use the books as a part of a systemwide learning program—supported by video and other media based on the content in the books. Still others work with Crisp Learning to customize the material to meet their specific needs and reflect their cultures. Regardless of how it is used, we hope you will join the more than 20 million satisfied learners worldwide who have completed a *Fifty-Minute Book*.

Preface

When *Working Together* first appeared over a dozen years ago, it was a first attempt to provide hands-on tools for individuals and groups dealing with the new realities of the diverse workplace signaled by the *Workforce 2000 Report*. The year 2000 has come and gone, and despite enormous progress, many issues of diversity still persist, while new ones have appeared to challenge us.

This third edition responds to the most recent shifts in diversity thinking, as well as the new challenges we face in this millennium, both domestically and in the new global economy. The effects of globalization and the events of September 11, 2001, are felt around the world and diversity can no longer be simply a domestic concern. Diversity consciousness and competence will play a crucial role in the contributions of organizations and individuals to a stable economic system and world peace.

We must include and support all kinds of groups and individuals if diversity is to unite us rather than divide us, and if we are to realize the bottom-line benefits to both business and society of respecting and making use of the ideas, talents, and spirit of a diverse population.

Several acknowledgments are in order. The important contributions of Amy Zuckerman, my colleague and friend, to the second edition of this book still shine through this new edition. In addition, a public word of thanks is overdue to Mike Crisp who has personally encouraged and advised this author over the years and editions. In particular, I am grateful to Debbie Woodbury whose editorial prompting and timely support has brought this edition to market.

George F. Simons
Principal
George Simons International

Contents

Part 4: Taking Action

Part 5: Diversity and Globalization

Part 6: Conclusion

Introduction

Diversity is the reality, the promise, and the challenge of our world and our workplace. We hoped that a new millennium would bring about peace and prosperity at home, at work, and throughout the world. In 2001, we sadly discovered that we still have much to do to keep the dream of diversity alive. This will take all of our diverse skills, talents, insights, and efforts. The task starts with each of us personally.

Working with people who look, believe, speak, or act differently can be awkward and uncomfortable. You don't know what to say, or what to expect. You find yourself inhibited, self-conscious, or even fearful. Some people don't react or behave as you expect. Perhaps you do your best to treat everyone equally and fairly, but others tell you that you are insensitive, unfair, or prejudiced. Perhaps some have even accused you of discriminating against them. If you are an "outsider" in a culture not your own, you may be angry or frustrated about not being taken seriously.

The future will bring more diversity, not less. It will challenge leaders all over the world to draw out the unique gifts of each person or group in order to reach common goals. You can champion diversity, whether you manage a multinational corporation, are a government employee, or simply work side by side with another person who is different from you.

Working Together helps you to understand and respect other people and to gain understanding and respect from them. You will learn to:

> ➤ **Manage your mind**—master how you think about yourself and others.

> ➤ **Manage your words**—speak and listen effectively to people of other backgrounds.

> ➤ **Manage your unspoken language**—know how to pay attention to the messages you send by "where, when, and how" you do things.

So, pick up your pencil—this is both a "read" and a "do" book—and let's begin!

WHAT DO I WANT TO LEARN?

In the list below, check (✔) the goals that are important to you. Focus on them as you read this book. This will help you see and appreciate the progress you make as you learn.

I want to:

- ❏ Manage a diverse workforce better than I do now.

- ❏ Work effectively with people of other backgrounds.

- ❏ Avoid offending those different from me.

- ❏ Avoid taking offense when people speak or act in unfamiliar or unexpected ways.

- ❏ Feel more secure around people whose values, opinions, and priorities differ from mine.

- ❏ Understand, appreciate, and gain cooperation from those who talk and act differently.

- ❏ Build an organization that gets 100% from 100% of its people.

- ❏ Influence the decision makers to treat others more fairly.

- ❏ Combat prejudice and injustice.

- ❏ Be clear about my values about cultural diversity and put them into practice.

- ❏ Become more comfortable visiting or living within other cultures.

I also want to:

_____

_____

X

Manage Your Mind

Which Side Is Up?

Below is a map of the world—upside down! This map, called the Peters Projection, gives a more objective picture of the size of the world's continents and nations in relation to each other than traditional versions.

Can you pinpoint where you are now, or where your parents and your ancestors came from? Where are the "roots" of some of your neighbors and co-workers?

Practice

How does this view of the world change the importance of certain continents and countries? How does it feel to look at the world from a different point of view?

It occurs to me that:_____

_____

_____

_____

_____

_____

*For more information about how maps affect our thinking, go to www.diversophy.com/maps.htm

Who's in the Center of Our Universe?

Three hundred years ago people argued over whether the earth or the sun was the center of the universe. When science eventually proved that the earth revolved around the sun, many people found it hard to believe.

It is easy to take a one-sided view and assume that how we see things is the way everybody sees them. The word used to describe this attitude is *ethnocentric*. However, there are many cultures and countless unique individuals. The world actually has as many midpoints as there are people to look out from them.

We often say that to understand other people we need to "walk a mile in their shoes," but this is not always easy. You can study others, talk and listen to them, or even try to imagine and feel like they do, but your eyes, ears, and mind still relate everything to your own background and experiences. Still it is worth a try. The exercise below will help you do this.

Practice

Think of someone who is hard for you to relate to. What makes this person different? Think especially of the things that bother you about this person.

Now shift your point of view. Imagine you are in this person's body and mind. You now have his or her eyes, thoughts, and feelings. Imagine that this person is at the center of the world and is looking out at you. What do you think that he or she might find irritating or hard to understand or accept about you:

1. _____

2. _____

3. _____

Good try! But, really you won't know for sure how another person sees you unless you ask, and he or she is willing to tell you. However, you just did something really important. You stepped out of the center of your world. You let yourself see things from someone else's point of view. Practice this. Try this with some of the people you encounter tomorrow, especially those you find hard to understand. If you can do this, you have learned and started to use one of the most basic diversity skills.

What Makes People Different?

Biology

No two people, other than identical twins, have the same genes. Biology determines our sex and the color of our skin, hair, and eyes. Biology can also limit us, as when a person is born with a physical or mental disability.

Most biological differences don't mean much in themselves. It's what people make of them that really counts. This means we need to look at another kind of difference: culture.

Culture

Think of culture as the sum total of how we are taught to think and to behave by our family and society. We imagine, make, do, and celebrate things according to the rules of our culture. Culture tells us who we are and tells us how to think and feel about those who are different from us. Our culture directs us in what to believe and hold dear, and tells us how to act in various situations to protect those things. It is the lens through which we see things and interpret what they mean, and it is the tool we use to learn to survive and succeed in our part of the world.

When you belong to several different groups, you are actually a member of several different cultures. These cultures are like layers on a cake.

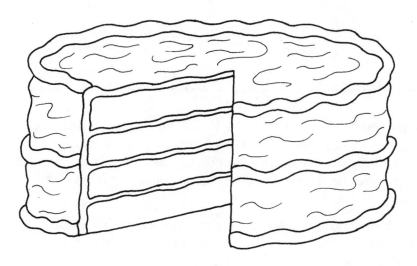

Seeing and Valuing My Cultures

With all the groups or cultures we belong to, we are like slices of cake with many layers. Each of our layers teaches us something about how to understand everyday events and how to behave. These layers make us sometimes like other people, sometimes different from them.

Picture yourself as the slice of cake below. Write on each layer some of the things that make you different from other people at work or in your neighborhood. Start with the basics like gender, race, where you or your ancestors came from, religion, and so on.

Practice

What are the layers on your cake?

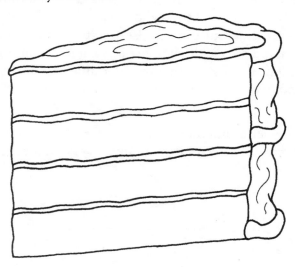

Everyone has his or her own set of biological and cultural differences. Also, each of us has a personal history that sets us apart from other people. Some cultures celebrate this individuality more than others. For example, some people celebrate by lighting candles on a birthday cake. Some cultures hide little treasures in the cake for lucky guests to find.

If you like, draw a candle on your cake as a reminder that you bring a special light into the world. Or, make a little drawing of a treasure that you feel represents something good about one of your cultures.

HOW AM I DIFFERENT?

Though we usually think of others as different from us, it is just as true that we are different from them. Below are some common ways we differ from each other. Each is followed by an unfinished phrase or two that can help us see how we think about these differences. Read each description and finish the phrase. Don't search for a correct answer. Just write the first response that comes to mind—that is how your culture talks to you. You may have second thoughts about what your culture tells you. Write those down, too.

Gender: Because we are born male or female the world treats us differently. The culture in which we are raised teaches us how to be feminine or masculine.

A real man is _____

_____

A real woman is _____

_____

Family: The family group has its own rhythms, customs, and rituals.

At home we usually _____

_____

Our family celebrates _____

_____

Age: The generation we grow up in experiences the world in its own unique way.

People of my age _____

_____

CONTINUED

Race: Categories that a society may create to classify people by their color, appearance, and other traits.

I am seen as belonging to _____ race because _____

_____

Nationality and Ethnicity: How we identify ourselves as citizens of a country, or as a people with a common heritage, culture, belief, or language.

As a _____ I learned _____

_____

Geography, Region: Distinctions we make about ourselves based on the part of a country we live in or come from.

Where I come from, people _____

_____

Organization: Ways we do and see things as a result of working together in a specific group or company.

In our organization we _____

_____

Belief: How we see ourselves because of our religion or philosophy of life. Having a common faith or personal conviction about who we are and why we are in this world makes us similar to some people and different from others.

People like me believe _____

_____

Before going on, read over what you have written in this exercise. Then go back to your slice of cake on page 6 and jot down at least one benefit you get, or strength you have, from being part of each of your cultural groups.

WE ARE THE ONES WHO MAKE DIFFERENCES IMPORTANT

Cultural differences become important because of the emphasis we put on them. People pay more attention to some differences than to others and make them more important. Here are some more differences that were not listed on pages 7 and 8. In your opinion, how important do people in your community or workplace regard these differences? Rate each as:

1 = not important; 2 = somewhat important; or 3 = very important

_____ **Occupation/Profession:** How we identify ourselves as a result of the kind of work we do. (Engineer, tradesperson, machinist, retailer, artist, marketer, supervisor, etc.)

_____ **Sexual Orientation:** The choices we are inclined to make about those we want as sexual partners, or the choice not to have sexual partners. (Gays, lesbians, heterosexuals, bisexuals, celibates.)

_____ **Social Class:** How others see us, and how we see ourselves, through family status, income, education, or lifestyle. (Rich, poor, middle class, high school or university education, etc.)

_____ **Looks and Disabilities:** How we judge body size and shape, structural or functional differences, or differing physical or mental abilities. (Tall, short, heavy, thin, hearing-impaired, paraplegic, etc.)

With these distinctions in mind, read a newspaper or listen to a news broadcast. Notice how many stories involve cultural differences either directly or just below the surface. Notice how, when reading or listening, you sometimes automatically judge others because of their race, gender, social class, occupation, nationality, physical make-up, sexual orientation, age, or beliefs.

Culture Is in Our Language

Culture lives in our language. How people speak usually reflects the culture they come from. But culture is also found in how we spontaneously talk to ourselves, both consciously and unconsciously. For example, does your mind prefer to speak in words, pictures, sounds, or feelings?

Our culture is always talking to us whether we notice it or not. The very instant we hear or see something or someone, we begin to talk to ourselves. Our minds go to work trying to answer two questions:

> *What does this mean?*

> *What should I do about it?*

We automatically look in our cultural mental library or database for the best answers we can find. This is why we have opinions about everything—without even trying! Culture is always talking to us and through us.

What We Say to Ourselves

How does your culture show up in your thinking?

As you look at each word or phrase on the following page, listen to the conversation that starts in your mind. In the column "What I Visualize," describe briefly the first word, picture, or scene that pops into your mind. In the next column, jot down how you first judged each item. Did what you get feel good or bad, beautiful or ugly, true or false? Notice that you really do have an opinion about everything. Use the last column to note where you got your idea or feeling or at least where you think it came from.

Remember, you are neither good nor bad because of what your mind and your culture automatically say to you. This is how they are meant to work. What you do with these thoughts later is what counts. Two people may have completely different responses, as the example for "immigrant" shows.

Word	What I Visualize	Judgments	Source
immigrant	A person on a boat An unshaven worker	Good, brave Bad, they scare me	My grandmother's stories My dad avoided them
money			
home			
foreigners			
management			
working woman			
artist			
death penalty			
white men			
unions			
gay or lesbian			
college			
marriage			
work			

Who Influences You?

Clearly, our minds do not work in the same way.

➤ Grover believes the death penalty keeps people from committing crimes—he grew up in a lawless environment where people felt very angry and vengeful about threats to their well-being. Karin disapproves and believes it incites violence—she comes from a country with little or no violence and no death penalty.

➤ Nikki, whose mother was a lawyer, likes the idea of women having careers outside the home—she feels enriched by it. Fran was educated to be a homemaker and a mother. She thinks that part-time work can be okay for women, but is afraid a full-time career would hurt family life.

Practice

Our minds are anchored in both our personal and our common past. While this helps us make sense of things, it can also keep us from understanding and working with each other.

When you were growing up, whose words and actions made you fear, suspect, or avoid people who were different from you? Does anyone reinforce those same feelings now? Write down what you learned earlier that you would like to change now.

_____

_____

_____

During your youth, who helped you to be curious about new things and different people? What did they say and do? Jot down some of the things that you would like to imitate or initiate.

_____

_____

_____

Is It One or Many?

More than 2,000 years ago, philosophers identified four basic questions that our minds automatically ask to help us understand our experiences and how to handle them:

1. Is it one or many?

2. Is it good or evil?

3. Is it true or false?

4. Is it beautiful or ugly?

Some version of these questions is found in all cultures and languages. Every human mind asks such questions automatically. They go beyond any one subject. We apply them instinctively to everything we think about.

The mental question, "Is it one or many?" is not easy to grasp at first, but it is important when working with people who are different from us. Here are some examples of how we see what belongs together and what doesn't, or decide what's the same and what's different.

➤ Harvey lives in a big city. For him all snow is the same—pretty to look at, but a nuisance to walk on and to drive in.

➤ Moira, who lives next door to Harvey, is a skier. She refers to snow as "popcorn," "powder," "mashed potatoes," or "ice," and knows how to ski on each type.

Because of our background, we see some things in more detail than others:

➤ For Lucia, the computer is simply an accounting tool.

➤ Baz, an electrical engineer, sees a computer as a complex device made up of many interacting parts.

The same is true about how we look at people:

➤ Sukirno, a postal worker who lives in Sumatra, sees Indonesians as more than 300 different peoples.

➤ Jane, who works in a department store in London, thinks all "Asians" look and act the same.

By asking, "Is it one or many?" our minds try to figure out what or who fits together and what or who does not. When we answer this question, we either include or exclude others from a group according to our cultural standards and experience. We not only separate "us" from "them," but we decide how we are alike and how we are different.

We can choose to be separated by our cultural differences or use them to enrich and expand our minds and our lives. We can also see how we all belong to the larger human family. When it comes to people, there are ways in which we are one and ways in which we are many.

Prejudging Others—Everybody Does It

If you look only from the center of your cultural "solar system," your mind will automatically conclude that:

➤ The world consists of "us" and "them."

➤ We are right, they are wrong.

➤ We are good, they are bad.

➤ We are beautiful, they are ugly.

As a result, it is not uncommon to find one group persecuting another because they see the other as less than human, morally inferior, technologically backward, or not having "the true faith." Prejudice appears when a person rejects others on the basis of, "I wouldn't want my sister to marry one," or "Some of my best friends are _____, but..."

Learning how our minds judge others before we really know them is a first step in managing prejudice. We can turn our opinions, feelings, and preferences into "facts" simply by the way we talk about others. We say things like "The sales group is too noisy," rather than, "I'm having difficulty concentrating when so many people are talking at once." Or "Arabs are too pushy," rather than "I get uncomfortable when Hakim speaks and gestures so close to me." Judgments lead us to want to label others.

Prejudice starts when we interpret what we experience (something subjective) as an absolute truth about others (something objective). We start to believe in these "truths" and spread them to other people. "Bias" is what results when we act out our prejudices towards others without examining our prejudices.

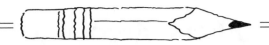

REVERSE PREJUDICIAL THINKING

Let's reverse the process we use to create stereotypes and biases against others. Change each statement below about a group to a more subjective statement about what the person might have been thinking or feeling when he or she made the statement.

Women are too emotional. _____

_____

U.S. Americans are too individualistic. _____

_____

Hispanics stick to themselves too much. _____

_____

If you are working alone, here is another thing you can do. Ask yourself what you say about other people or groups. Change two of your prejudices or stereotypes into statements about yourself.

1. What I say about them: _____

_____

What I'm actually saying about me: _____

_____

2. What I say about them: _____

_____

What I'm actually saying about me: _____

_____

Resisting New Information About Others

Our minds have what psychologists call a "confirmation bias." When we see something unfamiliar or meet someone who is different, we try to conform or fit this new information into old categories, to combine what we learn with what we already know. This is one way that our minds help us understand things. However, we can easily use this same process to ignore the facts, or to change new data about a person or a situation to agree with what we think we already know.

If we learned to think of a certain group of people as lazy, we particularly notice when they are late, while ignoring people from other groups who may also be tardy. If we believe people of a certain culture are stingy or greedy, we will see them only taking, and are likely to ignore when they are giving. What we believe of them becomes true for us, simply because we believe it and look for it.

Prejudice is a self-fulfilling prophecy! Our minds have places for certain kinds of people, and work hard to keep them there.

Filling in the Blanks

Our minds also like to fill in the blanks. Maybe that's why some people like puzzles so much, or why as children we enjoyed gazing at the stars or the clouds and making pictures and stories out of them.

Practice

Look at the symbols drawn below and notice how your mind tries to fill in the blanks to make sense out of what they are trying to say.

Write whatever message you think this line of symbols might contain.

_____

_____

_____

Compare your answer to the author's suggested
response in the back of the book.

Bob Abramms of ODT Inc., a publisher of diversity resources, has observed how our tendency to fill in the blanks produces a "halo" effect. We assume that people who are good at one thing will be good at something else. For example, we expect an accountant to manage his or her personal finances well, or a kind and indulgent manager to be good with children. We do the reverse as well—expecting a person who is bad at one thing to be bad at something else, for example, thinking that a factory worker who reads poorly will not understand machines either. Sometimes we even go beyond this to infer that a person of a different culture who fails at a part of his or her job is simply inferior and will not succeed at anything. Putting either good or bad halos around others keeps us from seeing them as they are.

When we catch our minds filling in the blanks, we need to remind ourselves of how little we know about others and then try to find out more. So, we see that several very normal mental functions are the source of what we call prejudice. Our minds "pre-judge" things—it's unavoidable. Without prejudging, we would have so many decisions to make we would be unable to cope with life.

In some matters, we can afford to be slightly wrong and still come out okay. But, if our minds have false information about people, or we simply don't know enough to make good judgments and we act without seeking more information, this can cause us to be unfair.

So, it is up to us to keep our prejudices from harming others by how we think and act. In the end, our unchecked prejudices make us the real losers. Our lives become narrow and we miss out on new ideas and fresh ways of looking at things. When we reject or despise others, we usually reject or despise parts of ourselves. We "put down" others in an effort to make ourselves feel more important. In the long run, this only makes us feel worse about ourselves. Prejudice is a double-edged sword and the sharper edge is likely to cut the one who swings it.

Practice

What have you missed out on because you judged someone unfairly or too quickly? Write a sentence about it below. You might think about how you might reverse the situation if possible.

My missed opportunity:

_____

_____

_____

_____

_____

_____

CASE STUDY: How Do You Manage Cultural Discomfort?

Our cultural differences show up in what our minds tell us about ourselves and about others. Much of this can take place without our noticing it. The silent mind works unconsciously and causes us to react automatically or habitually with feelings and sometimes with actions. This happens, for example, when we perceive people doing things that make their differences stand out. Look at the following examples and ask yourself how you might be affected in similar situations.

Lee Ming is embarrassed when she must talk to Lester, a subordinate who lost an arm. She does not know how to look at him or how to talk about his disability. As a result, she rushes through their meetings and avoids giving Lester feedback that she fears might be hard for him to take.

How do I think, feel, or react to a person with a disability?

_____

_____

Hans, who is white, feels afraid when negotiating with his supervisor Henry, who is black. Henry is a much larger man than Hans and when Henry talks to Hans he seems to stare. Hans finds himself avoiding Henry except when absolutely necessary.

My reaction to someone of a different race:

_____

_____

Hector is a personnel officer. Whenever a woman he thinks is beautiful arrives for an interview, he automatically puts on his "charming gentleman act." He finds later that he did not pay attention to parts of the interview and his report is inaccurate. The woman doesn't get hired, or gets hired for the wrong job.

How I respond to a person who is attractive to me:

_____

_____

Kalid becomes angry when several of his co-workers talk among themselves in their native language. He suspects they are talking and laughing about him or just wasting time. He finds himself being irritable and avoiding them. He complains about them to others.

How I react to people who speak a different language around me:

_____

_____

Juanita is charmed by Luc's French accent on the telephone. Even though they have never met and their dealings are strictly business, she spends much more time on Luc's reports than she does on those of the other overseas agents.

How another's accent can affect me:

_____

_____

Note: The case studies on pages 20–21 should be done individually and privately. The author does not recommend sharing their results in group training.

EXPAND YOUR COMFORT ZONE

This exercise will help you look at how you interact with people who make you uncomfortable, cause you stress, leave you less effective, or lead you to act unfairly. If you find it hard to think of situations, ask people who see you interact with others and whom you trust to tell you how they see you. You might want to photocopy this page to use again to improve your comfort level with another group.

With whom am I uncomfortable? What type of person disturbs me in some way?

_____

When dealing with such people, what causes me to react negatively?

_____

What reactions do I have? What do I say to myself? How do I feel?

_____

On a scale of one to five, how much does this hinder me from working together with this person, or giving him or her fair treatment?

1 = little—when I notice it, I can usually put it aside

5 = lots—the situation seems to take over and I don't feel like I have any control over it or any skills to deal with it

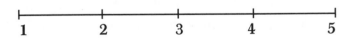

1	2	3	4	5

How might I change this? Who might give me information, feedback, or support?

_____

_____

_____

The Good vs. the Bad

Most of us will feel either comfort or discomfort when we interact with someone of a different culture. The trick is not to allow ourselves to play favorites or treat others unfairly. Also, we can't assume that other people feel about us as we feel about them.

Did you ever look into a kaleidoscope?

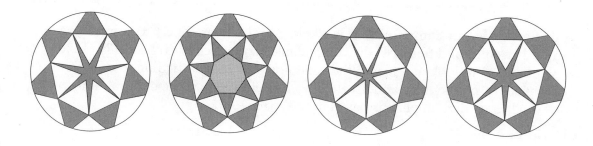

As the kaleidoscope turns, bits of glass fall into infinitely diverse patterns that are reflected by mirrors and form beautiful designs.

Practice

Occasionally we see the goodness and richness of human diversity in the same way. What are some things you have admired about people who are different from you?

_____

_____

_____

_____

Lines that Divide Us

Our everyday experience with others is complex. We are often annoyed by others' differences or we annoy them with ours. When we rub each other the wrong way we develop sore spots and pet peeves. When this happens, we may decide not to work with or hire another on the basis of "I'm just not comfortable with so-and-so." As a result, cultural differences cause us to build walls around ourselves and act unfairly to those outside our walls.

Practice

Look around your community or workplace and you are likely to see race, sex, and other cultural differences dividing people economically and socially. Take a few moments to look at a few of the economic and social dividing lines in your workplace or community and list them to the left. Identify the cultural difference on which each dividing line is based in the space to the right.

Dividing Line

In my workplace almost all the lower-level support staff jobs are held by women.

Cultural Difference

Gender—male vs. female

It is hard to get people to change the everyday realities of social injustice, or the violence and crime associated with both poverty and wealth. Fear often causes us to build the walls around us a little higher, and keeps us from bringing our many talents together to create a better world and workplace.

Turning Fear into Curiosity

We can manage our prejudices better if we can turn our fear into curiosity. Curiosity can lead to new possibilities. Curiosity and excitement are the opposite of fear and anxiety. Imagine two people standing in line to ride a roller coaster; both have sweaty palms and churning stomachs, yet one is excited and the other is terrified. Some people are stimulated by a new job; others are frightened by it. How do we move from fear to excitement? Some differences, for example sexual orientation or race, are particularly terrifying to some people.

Because curiosity is fed by the same energy as fear, we can transform one emotion into another more easily than we think. We do this by changing how we talk to ourselves. The best way to succeed is to ask ourselves "What if . . . " and coming up with new possibilities.

What if we could get beyond our differences? Use the image below to note some of your fears about other people, and then turn them into fresh possibilities by envisioning, "What if . . ."

How can we do this more often? We can ask about things we don't understand. We can take risks a little at a time. People sometimes say, "Curiosity killed the cat." But, they also notice that, "A cat has nine lives." Like cats we can take risks carefully, and if we occasionally have a bad experience, we will probably survive it!

---

*For an excellent book on this topic, read *Managing Personal Change* by Cynthia Scott and Dennis T. Jaffe, Crisp Publications.

Review

What are the important things you have learned thus far?

_____

_____

_____

_____

What things might you want to do differently as a result of what you have learned?

_____

_____

_____

_____

Turn back to page ix and review the goals you set for yourself there. How would you change or add to what you would like to get out of this workbook now?

Manage Your Words

Name-Calling

Spoken words reflect how we think. They have a great impact on how we get along or don't get along with each other. In this section, we will look at words as the basic tools with which we try to understand each other and create agreements that work.

Practice

Some of the names that people give to cultural groups are disrespectful, or have become so over time. What are some names that have been given to cultural groups to which you belong? Which of these are uncomfortable for you and which are okay?

Name	Not Okay	Okay
Example: They called me a "Girl"	☑	❑
_____	❑	❑
_____	❑	❑
_____	❑	❑
_____	❑	❑
_____	❑	❑

People sometimes use disrespectful names for other groups out of ignorance. They either don't know how the people want to be called or don't understand how sensitive others are to certain names.

If someone unknowingly calls someone by a name you don't like, speak up. Tell them how you feel in a way that will help them to make a change without blaming them. Make sure you let others know which names your cultural group is comfortable with.

Sometimes we tend to get a little too thick-skinned for our own good. We grow to accept names that demean us and the cultural group to which we belong. We allow ourselves to be called "girl," or "kid," or tolerate a racial or ethnic nickname that is unflattering. We must think enough of ourselves, and people like us, to insist on a change.

Review the list you made on page 29 and circle any inappropriate names you have come to accept. What names are used for other cultural groups where you live and work? Are these names acceptable to the people to whom they refer? Is it acceptable for you to use them? What are the right names? If you don't know, ask!

Practice

Using the space below, find correct names for the groups of people you work with and speak about.

Names Used   **Appropriate Name**

_____   _____

_____   _____

_____   _____

If you have called someone by an inappropriate name, either inadvertently or in a time of stress or anger, don't defend your mistake or give excuses—just apologize! Then find a way to remind yourself not to make the same mistake again.

Individuals have the right to decide what they want to be called. If you don't know, it is up to you to ask. This goes for people's personal names, too. This list will help you. Check (✔) the boxes of the items you need to act on:

❑ Can I pronounce others' names correctly (that is, as they do)?

❑ Do I know how people are politely addressed in their own language and the right time to use a family name or a given name?

❑ Am I aware of the order in which people of various cultures write or speak their family and given names? Some cultures give many names, some only a few, and others a single one.

❑ Do I know the titles of respect that go with others' names and the right time to use them?

❑ Do I avoid the use of impersonal slang names, such as "Honey," "Dear," "Babe," "Mama," "Sweetheart," "Fella," "Guy," "Mac," and "Ace," that may annoy people?

Use Humor Appropriately

Humor is one of our greatest human assets. It helps us cope with tense situations and can open up a fresh point of view. Humor, in the form of irony, satire, ridicule, or stereotyping can also be a powerful social weapon. Think of some of the devastating political cartoons you have seen in newspapers.

Good workplace humor helps us laugh with people, not at them. Here are some simple hints for using humor in multicultural situations.

Laughing with Each Other

Life is full of funny events and touching moments. Being able to laugh at ourselves and our predicaments endears us to one another. The best stories are those you can tell about yourself in such a way that others can recognize a piece of themselves, and you can laugh together.

Living and working in a multicultural setting will get you into many laughable situations. Remember the first time you tried something that was foreign to you? For example, the first time you used chopsticks, or used a bathroom in a strange culture, or showed up in the wrong place at the wrong time! Knowing how to laugh at yourself helps you see that your own cultural outlook is only one of many ways to see the world.

Laughing at Each Other

Don't tell ethnic jokes or stories that make fun of a person's gender or culture. Almost all of these jokes make some group of people feel inferior. They exaggerate stereotypes of how people look and act. Few are very original.

Sexual humor, more often than not, degrades both women and men, and may bring charges of sexual harassment, even from casual bystanders.

Telling ethnic or sexual jokes is like name-calling. It is frequently used to bond a group and keep outsiders in their place. It may make us feel good about ourselves for a few moments while we laugh at others, but unconsciously it deepens stereotypes and negative views of others. It also tells the world that we are so insecure about ourselves that we need to put others down to feel okay.

In multicultural environments, and in times of change and stress, people become very sensitive. Unless you're confident that the jokes you tell won't offend any group at all, don't tell them!

Practice

How would you handle a joke at work that was unfair to you or to another cultural group? Check (✔) the approach you find best.

I would:

❏ 1. Ignore the joke and go on with business, but take the joke-teller aside later and tell him or her my feelings.

❏ 2. Take the storyteller to task right then and there, in public.

❏ 3. Tell an appropriate joke to model the kind of jokes that should be told.

❏ 4. Laugh now but tell the joke-teller about my discomfort later in private.

❏ 5. Tell an even worse joke about a group to which the joke-teller belongs.

Compare your answers to the author's responses in the back of the book.

*For an excellent book on this topic, read *Making Humor Work* by Terry Paulson, Crisp Publications.

Teasing

Teasing takes place when we use a little bit of aggression to show affection for another person. As with joke telling, it is important to avoid ethnic and cultural overtones. Men tend to tease more often than women.

Some teasing consists of rather strong put-downs. Men of some cultures bond with each other by trading insults, yet such talk may be totally misunderstood by women and other cultural groups.

Rita Risser, author of *How to Work with Men,* suggests a four-step strategy you can use if you find yourself a victim of the "Insult Game."

➤ First, recognize that it is a game.

➤ Second, observe carefully until you know the rules.

➤ Third, sharpen your wits and play along.

➤ Finally, accompany your jab with a smile.

Risser's advice will probably work for the way the game is played in most cultures. Wherever you are, making sure you know the rules is crucial. In today's workplace, however, one must be extremely careful to avoid what others may feel is harassment.

Just Like a Man!

Today more than ever, women are unhappy with the traditional male focus at work and in social situations. Frustration with this system sometimes turns into hostility toward men. This surfaces in sarcastic humor, ridiculous stereotypes, and cutting remarks about men as men. Now that diversity stresses inclusion of everyone, this needs to stop. If you are a man, here are some ways to deal with the situation:

Manage Your Mind

➤ Recognize that you personally have not created the system in which women and men find themselves today.

➤ Laugh at yourself when you do fall into one of the male stereotypes.

➤ Put yourself in the shoes of women and other groups. Listen carefully to hear the real needs behind the sarcasm and wisecracks.

Manage Your Words and Actions

➤ Use what power you have to change things that are unfair.

➤ Don't expect a lot of sympathy for male dilemmas. Your best source of understanding and support will come from other men who are aware of the problems of cultural and gender diversity.

➤ Realize that in some cases men too may experience harassment. Know what steps to take if you feel this is happening.

For more about male and female behavior in the workplace, read *Men and Women, Partners at Work* by George Simons and G. Deborah Weissman, Crisp Publications.

The "Ouch!" Technique

Here is a trick that can help members of a team or group become more aware of each other's cultural sensibilities and sore spots. Get the individuals in your group to agree to call out the word "Ouch!" when someone in the group says or does something offensive. Unless what has been said or done is so painful that it keeps the group from going on, or the purpose of the group is to discuss tension between cultures, don't stop to talk about the incident. Getting deeply into feelings and sensibilities when you have another agenda can turn into attacking, defending, or deciding who's right or wrong instead of doing the task at hand.

Saying "Ouch!" teaches us where each other's cultural and personal boundaries lie, and how to respect them.

Practice

Think of a common situation that is an "Ouch!" for you and jot it down here.

_____

_____

_____

_____

_____

_____

How to Bridge the Language Barrier

Most of us are truly fluent only in our mother tongue. Unless we learned more than one language as a child, it is rare for us to speak flawlessly in a second language. However, education, training, and experience also give us different languages. Software engineers speak "computerese," attorneys speak "legalese," and construction workers talk "hardhat."

When people are speaking different languages (or using unfamiliar jargon) in the workplace, it can easily lead to misunderstanding. Here are some ways to avoid this situation. How good are you at putting them into practice?

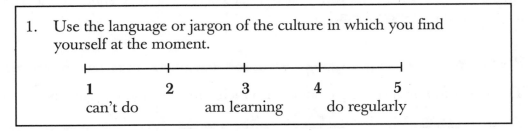

1. Use the language or jargon of the culture in which you find yourself at the moment.

1	2	3	4	5
can't do		am learning		do regularly

Being forced to learn the language of the majority has sometimes been a way of oppressing minorities. Choosing to learn someone else's language doesn't mean you have to give up your own or value it less.

When you are a visitor where people do not speak your language, immediately start to learn some simple phrases for everyday interactions. Knowing how to say "Hello," "Goodbye," Please," "Thank you," and so on in another person's language, can go a long way toward creating good will. But, don't stop there!

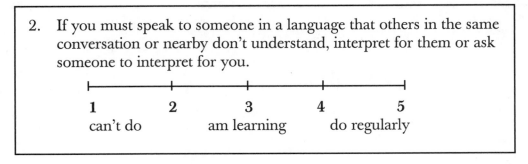

2. If you must speak to someone in a language that others in the same conversation or nearby don't understand, interpret for them or ask someone to interpret for you.

1	2	3	4	5
can't do		am learning		do regularly

If the conversation seems too unimportant to relate word for word, stop from time to time to give others the gist of what you are discussing in your language.

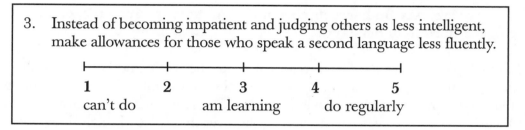

3. Instead of becoming impatient and judging others as less intelligent, make allowances for those who speak a second language less fluently.

1	2	3	4	5
can't do		am learning		do regularly

Besides being patient, it will help if you speak more slowly, use simple words and avoid slang. It is usually not helpful to try to imitate the other person's limited use of the language (for example, by speaking "broken English" or using "baby talk"). It is particularly offensive to raise your voice and speak louder, as if the other person were hearing impaired, when they simply do not understand your words or your accent.

Realize that thinking and speaking in a foreign language can be as tiring as hard physical work. It is important to notice when people are beginning to tire and provide breaks. If you are the one speaking someone else's tongue, be sure to tell them when they are going too fast or when your concentration is beginning to fade.

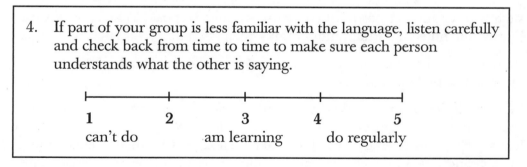

4. If part of your group is less familiar with the language, listen carefully and check back from time to time to make sure each person understands what the other is saying.

1	2	3	4	5
can't do		am learning		do regularly

Simply repeating back in your own words what you heard or asking the other person, "Could you tell me how you understand what we have said so far?" will help you check on how well you are communicating.

*For a great book on listening, read *The Business of Listening,* by Diana Bonet, Crisp Publications.

When We Speak the Same Language Differently

We may automatically judge a person's speech, his or her accent, rhythm, and pace, positively or negatively because they are different. For example:

> ➤ **We may find accents charming, mysterious, annoying, or simply hard to understand.**

Lloyd thinks Judith's flat Chicago accent makes her plain and boorish, while Judith thinks Lloyd's Oxford English makes him more intelligent than Chen, the chief engineer, whose Hong Kong English seems sing-songy and childish to her. Once they get to know each other, they discover that none of their views about each other are accurate.

> ➤ **They may sound too arrogant or too weak.**

Raj learned to use formal and indirect language when speaking to persons in authority. His new boss thinks that Raj lacks conviction about his ideas and is afraid to make decisions.

> ➤ **The pacing and timing may be different.**

Sheila is from New York City, where people normally talk over the ends of each other's sentences and find it stimulating. Jimmy is from Iowa, where people pause slightly after another has finished before starting to speak. When Sheila speaks to Jimmy, she finds him dull. Jimmy thinks Sheila is rude.

Remember once again that the judgments we make are usually just a reflection of our culture. Be fair to others!

When entering a conversation, try to match the pace and timing of the people with whom you are speaking. This may actually establish better rapport. Excellent salespersons often do this. They take their cues from their clients and match the ebb and flow of the clients' speech. Sometimes people learn a second language by reading and studying rather than conversing with native speakers. They are able to compose what they want to say, but fail to understand others well because of accent and pacing.

When Common Sense Isn't Common

When people share a culture, they understand many things that are unspoken. They understand what time to arrive for a meeting or for dinner. They know who should speak to whom and who shouldn't. They chat about some things and know what topics are too personal to discuss. However, when cultures mix, strange things happen. Common sense is no longer common.

Please bathe only within the bathtub as the bathroom floor has no drain.

Western visitors to Malaysia, for example, may be puzzled to find a sign like the one above in bathrooms of Western-style hotels. They assume that everyone showers or bathes in a bathtub. They may not realize that some cultures normally bathe outside a tub by pouring water over themselves and would find sitting in the water they are bathing in unsanitary and odd.

When people from different cultures mix, such as when large numbers of immigrants enter a country or a different group moves into a neighborhood, the bonds of common understanding are weakened. When diverse groups come together in the workforce or corporations merge, we can no longer assume that everybody shares the same unspoken language.

Newcomers often don't know the unwritten rules of the culture they enter, and locals often don't realize the newcomers have different values until something goes wrong, or someone is embarrassed. Think of your first day at a new job. Remember the worries and questions you had about where things were and how things were done. Now imagine the difficulty of entering a totally different culture.

Learning Each Other's Rules

When newcomers enter a neighborhood or organization, both sides become uncomfortable. We may get annoyed because we are used to having people understand us without having to be so explicit. On the other hand, if given explicit directions, we may find it impolite, or patronizing. We don't realize that we need to define what we want or mean. We become upset because "they" just don't "get it."

Practice

Think of when you began working with people from another culture or started a new job. What were some of the things that were difficult, uncomfortable, or embarrassing for you to tell others?

_____

_____

_____

Think of when you traveled to a different place, perhaps to another country, or when you visited with people from another culture. What were a few of the things that others felt you should have understood and were surprised, shocked, or amused to find that you didn't?

_____

_____

_____

Remember that practically speaking, the meaning of anything you say is what the other person understands. It doesn't matter what you intended to say; their response tells how they received the message. If another person is clearly not responding as you expected, you must do something else to get the message across. Becoming frustrated, angry, or blaming the other person wastes time and creates hard feelings.

How Words Work

Fortunately, despite the hundreds of languages and cultures, people do only a small number of things with language. Fernando Flores, co-author of *Understanding Computers and Cognition,* says there are four important things that people do when they speak.

1. We **ask** others to do things.

    Examples: *I want you to finish the budget by Friday noon.*
    I insist that you stay for the whole meeting.
    Please give me ten minutes.

2. We **promise** or refuse to do things.

    Examples: *I promise to meet you at the cafeteria at 7:00 tomorrow morning.*
    Yes, if you come to the shop tomorrow, I assure you, I'll be there.
    No, I will not consider this as part of my job.

3. We **assert** that certain things are true or false.

    Examples: *All the seats on this flight have been taken.*
    This metal part will not wear as well as a nylon one.
    I have evidence to show that we are losing sales in this market.

4. We **declare** or define an objective or goal, or proclaim a new **attitude or** state of affairs.

    Examples: *Anyone who smokes within the posted area will be reprimanded.*
    I apologize for neglecting to inform you as I promised.
    Thank you for reminding me.
    You're hired! You will supervise the team.
    I'm going to become a salesperson.

Practice

At the end of your next meeting, take a few minutes to reflect on which of the four kinds of speech came into play. Ask yourself:

- ❏ Did I ask something of the other person or they of me?

- ❏ Did I promise something to them or they to me?

- ❏ What did we tell each other about what is true or false?

- ❏ Did either of us commit ourselves to a new attitude, direction, definition, or state of affairs?

Keep these four questions in mind and use them as a checklist. If you can answer them fully and clearly after completing a business transaction with someone from a different culture, you will know what you have agreed upon.

In many cultures, how we create a solid relationship with others is more important than agreeing on the fine points. If we don't pay attention to the relationship, we may get no agreement at all!

Other ways people speak are sometimes not so easy to understand. Sometimes people deliberately create words or sound bites to sway people in one direction or another. When they do this for political purposes, it becomes propaganda. When they do it as art, it becomes poetry.

When Is an Agreement an Agreement?

Because of their differing cultural backgrounds, some people may see agreement where others see none. Therefore, it is important to check what kind of agreement you both expect when you begin to work together. Number each statement below from 1 (your most preferred) to 4 (your least preferred) form of agreement.

_____ We have a DEAL.

_____ We share a VISION.

_____ We have come to a LOGICAL SOLUTION.

_____ We UNDERSTAND and EMPATHIZE with each other.

Ask others with whom you frequently interact what kinds of agreements they prefer. Should they be spoken or written?

*From "The Transcultural Communicator," a communications and negotiations tool by Dr. George Simons and Dr. Walt Hopkins, found in *Global Competence*.

Cultural Double Binds

Some cross-cultural situations seem to put us in a no-win position. Here are some "double binds" and some tips about how to handle them.

1. Saying "No"

Wolf managed a team of Asian engineers in an overseas installation for his company. He laid out a project plan and explained it to the group. No one disagreed and they started to work. Four days into the project, Mori, one of the engineers, failed to produce the needed data for a critical part of the plan. Wolf was angry at Mori, who promised to do his best. Later a supervisor told Wolf that Mori had been at his computer workstation past midnight each night for the past four days.

In many cultures, saying "No" to someone's request or offer, even if it seems unreasonable, is impolite. The person may try to indicate something is wrong but signals they send may be too subtle to detect if you are not from that culture. People in these cultures may want to protect you or themselves from conflict or embarrassment, so they deliberately hold back.

In other cultures, "No" is never said to one in authority. The outsider who misses these signals may feel that an agreement has taken place and be surprised when a promise is not kept.

In yet other cultures, saying "No" is only a signal to renegotiate a better agreement. This may seem very impolite, even threatening to people from the first two kinds of cultures.

When in doubt, ask how disagreement is handled in the other person's culture. When dealing with people who are reluctant to say "No," check the agreement you think you made more than once, and look for signs of discomfort before going ahead. Clarify likely misunderstandings in private.

When dealing with someone who expects a "Yes" or "No" answer and such directness is uncomfortable for you, begin in low-risk situations and get feedback from someone who will tell you how you sound. When learning how to communicate in another culture, we often miss the finer points and overdo it. Feedback can help us "fine-tune" our language.

To what degree is saying "No" a problem between you and people from different cultures? Check (✔) the box below that describes your situation. Then, use the tips given here to jot down the strategy you would use to deal with it.

Saying "No"

❏ is not an issue   ❏ can be an issue   ❏ is a big issue

My strategy for dealing with saying "No" is _____

_____

 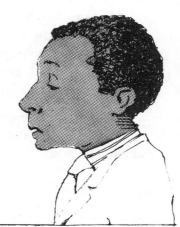

2. Politeness vs. Directness

Jeanne is conducting a technical training program for a multicultural group of assemblers in a high-tech production facility. Most who took her course gave her excellent ratings. She was feeling very good about her performance until supervisors complained that her trainees were unclear about several basic procedures.

Some people find it impolite to complain or to admit to others that they don't understand. To do so in their own culture would cause the other person to "lose face." To avoid embarrassment, problems are either subtly or indirectly communicated, or a third person is used as a go-between to carry the feedback or bad news.

More direct cultures may judge this as underhanded, cowardly, or a waste of time. They generally deal with a problem the moment it arises and assume the other person will not be offended. People from an indirect culture may find this uncivilized, disrespectful, or deliberately insulting. Sharing feelings too openly may look like insincerity to them.

Learn about the other person's culture. What do people in that culture tend to talk about and what do they tend to hold back? How direct are they? Find an informant, someone who knows both cultures well enough to explain things to you. Be slow to criticize or give feedback until you know how to do so in a way that the other can understand. Point out what is correct or what is working and then show how other things could be improved.

How big of a problem is politeness or directness for you and those with whom you live or work? Check (✔) the box, then use the tips given here to jot down a strategy for dealing with it.

Politeness vs. directness

❏ is not an issue   ❏ can be an issue   ❏ is a big issue

I would deal with it by _____

_____

3. Stress and Pressure

A task force has been formed to develop a strategic plan for organizing the company around a new product line. The task force includes participants from every level in the organization, and is to be a model for a new open attitude toward diversity in the company. As the deadline approaches, the senior managers start making decisions without consulting the junior members. When the junior members complain, they are labeled "young radicals" and told that they are poor team players. The junior members start holding caucuses of their own to deal with what they claim is dishonesty on the part of the senior managers.

Stress easily divides us into opposing groups that exert power and pressure over each other. We begin to deal with issues on a political rather than a personal level and blame people who are different for what is going wrong.

Avoid taking sides as much as possible. In culturally diverse groups we must learn to understand and value cultural differences, and be sensitive to different groups' particular needs. Often this diversity is just what is needed to solve the problem creatively.

If the group has become divided, try to create a safe forum where people can share ideas anonymously or air their differences without fear of reprisal. Take people aside one by one if necessary to create understanding.

Is stress and taking sides under pressure a problem between you and others with whom you live or work? Check (✔) the box that feels right to you, and, using the tips given here, jot down the strategy you would use to deal with it.

Sliding back into old behaviors and taking sides under pressure

❑ is not an issue   ❑ can be an issue   ❑ is a big issue

My strategy for dealing with it is _____

Culture and Politics Add Value to the Workplace

When we take sides on an issue or side with one group against the position of another, we are involved in politics. Most organizations are a strong mixture of culture and politics. Division may occur along many cultural lines—black and white, women and men, young and old, workers and management, straight and gay, sales and production, and so forth.

When groups are discriminated against or feels their integrity or interests are threatened, they will set out political objectives and fight for them. If they can find other groups with like interests, they may be able to create a coalition to increase their political power to get what they need. People from outside the group who sympathize and support the group are called "allies." Don't be afraid to be the ally of someone who is different from you when you feel it is right to do so.

The healthy organization has both a culture of its own and a political climate. Its culture unites people in the organization and helps it to focus, communicate, and achieve its goals. People are pulled together by their commitments to common values, goals, or benefits. These are reinforced by the rituals, rules, common language, and traditions that develop.

Political forces in the organization can bring vitality, and respond to, or speak for, change. They may be used to protect the diversity of human resources while guaranteeing the fair distribution of benefits within the organization. When they succeed they can make the organizational culture work for more people.

MY ORGANIZATION'S POLITICAL CLIMATE

In the space provided below, draw a picture or diagram of your group or organization. Include in it both the cultural factors that unify it, and the political issues that divide it.

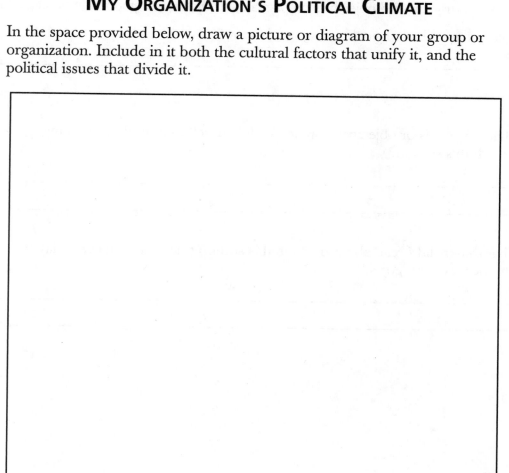

Where are you in this diagram? Put your initials wherever you see yourself contributing to the cultural values of the organization and also where you are clearly for or against an issue or political position. If you aren't involved, mark an X on the places where you could make a contribution.

Successful management of an organization requires skill at balancing the cultural forces and political forces that, if poorly managed, could tear it apart. Real leaders are able to bring out the diversity in people and put it to work for everybody's benefit.

Review

Review your goals and objectives on page ix and the update you made on page 26. What progress have I made on my goals so far?

_____

_____

What new goals or objectives might I set for myself as a result of working through this section?

_____

_____

What things did I read about or do in this section that I can use every day to help me reach my goals?

_____

_____

Manage the
Unspoken

Gestures and Body Language

Gestures often say more than words. Hand, arm, and head movements make it easier to say what we mean. Gestures are usually readily understood within one's culture, but may easily be misinterpreted by outsiders. No gestures are universal.

Even how one shakes one's head to indicate "yes" or "no," or waves a hand or arm to tell someone else to come closer, may differ significantly from culture to culture. A U.S. Peace Corps worker tells about asking a Bulgarian woman for a date and feeling rebuffed when she repeatedly shook her head from side to side. Her way of saying "yes" felt to him like "No," or "I'm not so sure!"

In his book, *Manwatching: A Field Guide to Human Behavior,* Desmond Morris points out how one familiar gesture, the circle made with thumb and forefinger may have totally different meanings in different cultures.

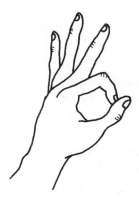

Possible meanings:

A-OK, everything's fine, perfect. (USA, UK, much of Europe)

He's a zero, don't take him seriously. Or, it's a zero, a failure. (France)

An obscene accusation. (Certain Mediterranean countries)

Please give me change in coins. (Japan)

Unconscious movements may say to others that we are comfortable or uncomfortable with them. We may appear rude or threatening, appealing, or even seductive—when we don't mean to be.

Something as simple as how we sit or cross our legs may send an unintended message. Europeans are sometimes unconsciously offended by the open way in which U.S. men cross their legs. For them it expresses a crude machismo. The U.S. men in turn, may suspect that European men who cross their legs in a closed way are effeminate.

Even smiles can mean different things. Some cultures smile a lot just to show they are friendly, others may see this as silly, false, or seductive. Some people laugh when they are embarrassed.

Was there a time when another person's gesture or body movement confused you, or you confused someone else by what you did or how you moved? Describe what happened in the space below:

_____

_____

_____

_____

These tips will help you become more alert to nonverbal cultural misunderstandings:

- ➤ **Pay attention to how others gesture or move.** If they are not from your culture, expect that their gestures may mean something slightly or even radically different from what you interpret.

- ➤ **Ask questions about gestures that puzzle you.** If your gesture is embarrassing, people may be reluctant to tell you, so ask someone you trust to tell you the truth. Be persistent. For example, men of one ethnic background may not be able to explain certain gestures that women of the same background make and vice versa, so you may have to ask more than one individual.

- ➤ **Don't imitate what you don't fully understand.** Doing so may invite misunderstanding or create offense.

- ➤ **Apologize if you make the wrong gesture or you misinterpret another's gesture.** Then ask for correct information.

- ➤ **Advise others who use gestures that could embarrass them or someone else.** Tell them in a way that does not make them "lose face."

Marking Time

When is "the right time?" People of different cultural backgrounds may give different answers to this question:

➤ At nine o'clock

➤ At twenty-one hundred hours

➤ At sunset

➤ When everything is ready

➤ When everyone is here

➤ When I'm good and ready

Some cultures count time like a digital watch. For them time is like money or some other commodity that can be used, saved, spent, or squandered. Others see only the rhythm, or cycles of growth of people or things.

We're not just talking about the gap between industrial and nonindustrial societies. Just walk from the research wing to the advertising offices of any large corporation and you can see a difference in the way people value time. Here is a story that a woman told about how she learned to be sensitive to another woman's experience of time.

When I was a supervisor, I had to discipline a woman who was a single parent for being late every day. She labeled me as a pushy boss who was unsupportive. She was angry and uncooperative and targeted me because she felt I didn't understand the needs of a single parent. We talked about her needs. Her son was always late for school, causing her to be late to work. So we brainstormed and discovered ways that she could get him ready on time.

DIFFERENT VIEWS OF TIME

Have you asked yourself any of these questions about time? Check (✔) those that sound familiar.

❏ How many meetings will it take to close the deal?

❏ What's her hurry?

❏ How long will they keep me waiting?

❏ How can I get his full attention? He always seems to be answering the phone or greeting visitors when I am meeting with him.

❏ Why doesn't she meet deadlines?

❏ How long do I have to be in this organization before I get to say something?

❏ Why not take the time to get everybody's opinion?

❏ If "time is money," how come I have so much time and so little money?

❏ When they say 9:00 A.M. do they mean "our" time or "their" time?

❏ How can somebody be so upset over a few minutes' difference?

❏ How can he expect me to remember something so far in advance?

❏ It's past and done. When will she stop bringing it up?

❏ Why is he calling me at this hour?

❏ Why is she sacrificing short-term profit for long-term considerations?

When you find yourself asking these questions, it's a good sign that different cultural values about time are at work.

What Is My Sense of Time?

How do I feel about time? How do I use it? Do I work in short brilliant spurts or move slowly but steadily? What do my culture and my organization say about time? Do they agree or disagree?

Practice

Mark yourself and your organization on the scale illustrated below:

Myself

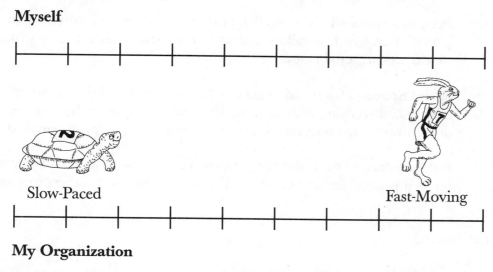

Slow-Paced   Fast-Moving

My Organization

How do you handle these differences? Here are some tips:

➤ Differences about time can be real and normal cultural differences. Don't jump to the conclusion that others are irresponsible or compulsive. On the other hand, don't assume that you are insensitive because you don't manage time the way they do.

➤ If you cannot adapt to the other person's sense of time, negotiate something that will work for both of you. Many organizations, for example, have adopted a system of flexible working hours, or provided child care and other conveniences to get the best out of their workforce.

➤ Remember that culture runs deep. It's one thing to make an agreement, and another to create a habit. Be patient and persistent with yourself and with others when you try to make changes.

Making Space

In his book *The Hidden Dimension,* Edward T. Hall points out that people have different kinds of space around them. These are:

> ➤ **Intimate Space**—This is our most private area. It lies within inches or centimeters of our body. We normally reserve this space for activity of the most intimate kind.

> ➤ **Personal Space**—This is usually a range of a meter or a yard or two. It is space into which we allow intimates and close friends, and in which we discuss personal matters.

> ➤ **Social Space**—This is the range in which we are usually comfortable talking and working with acquaintances or co-workers when we are doing impersonal business. It is roughly one to three meters or yards.

> ➤ **Public Space**—This is the range beyond social space. It extends out as far as it is possible for us to recognize and interact with others in some way.

It looks like this:

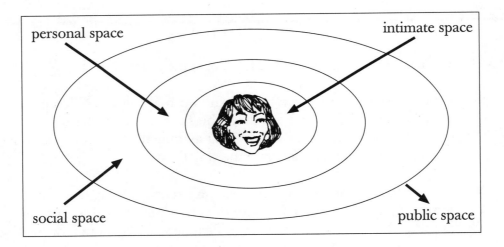

If you want to get a feel for what distances are right for you, pay attention to how close you get to others in various situations. Make notes on the diagram about what the distances are like for you.

How wide each type of space is for you will depend on your background and culture. Standing too close to someone may be interpreted as intruding, pushy, or "in your face." Standing too far away may be interpreted as cold, impersonal, afraid, or not interested. Sometimes circumstances change the rules for a short time and allow us to get closer (for example, when it's hard to hear—when machinery is running, or at a loud party).

The Solution

Learn to be flexible. Know that others may have different concepts of space than you do. When you meet people or enter into a conversation with them, stay put and let the other person adjust to you. Pay attention to what you are thinking if the distance between you seems uncomfortable.

If you want to become more informal or intimate, close the space between you very slowly, paying attention to the other person's reactions. If the other person seems too close to you, slowly move away until you are comfortable. See how the other person reacts.

Space at Work Checklist

When assigning, sharing, or arranging workspace with people different from yourself, the following checklist can help you.

- ❑ Be aware of what space may already mean to you and your co-workers. What does being in the middle, on the edge, having open or closed doors say to you and to them? What does it imply about authority, about how decisions are made, or about who talks to whom?

- ❑ Ask new people what kind of workspace they need to feel comfortable and give them time to settle in. Ask for workspace and time to settle in if you are the newcomer.

- ❑ Wherever necessary, agree on the boundaries of space and privacy that you and your co-workers need.

- ❑ On a new job have someone show you around the facility. Don't just ask where the bathrooms and cafeteria are. Inquire about the rules and customs. If you're introducing someone new, make sure you give the new person this information.

Touching Moments

Shana is about to present her research at a development committee meeting. Peter, her boss, puts his hand on her arm and keeps it there while he introduces her to the committee and praises her work. Shana feels humiliated. She felt that Peter's touch meant he was treating her like a "little girl" instead of letting her stand on her own. Peter, who was proud of Shana's work, felt he was helping her get off to a good start.

When people touch others physically it may mean different things. Touch may say:

➤ I have power and authority over you—cultural rules often allow the person with more power to touch those with less.

➤ Hello or goodbye—handshakes, backslaps, embraces, and kisses may be intimate in some cultures, casual in others.

➤ I want you to understand, accept, or pay attention to me—pats on the arm or shoulder, or holding hands will vary depending on a person's culture.

➤ I like you or want to become more intimate with you—affectionate, seductive, or sexual touches are often disguised and used in improper settings.

➤ I want to encourage or congratulate you—usually among peers. Hugs and embraces are sometimes mixed with power and authority, or sexual intention, often unconsciously.

➤ I am angry with you—using touch to express aggression is almost always inappropriate and dangerous.

➤ I want something from you—touching another to beg a favor is more acceptable in some cultures than others.

Warning: The gender and legal climate in many U.S. organizations discourages touching of any kind beyond a handshake. It may take some time before a new standard of reasonableness is in place. This is a risky area, particularly for new workers from more "touching cultures."

CASE STUDY: Privacy and How We Share Feelings

We often touch each other *without* using our hands or our bodies. We can be "touchy" about how we share our private feelings and even about how we make eye contact with one another. Cultures differ about what they consider public information, or things that are okay to ask others, and private information, which is only shared with family or intimates—or no one.

Following are four examples of how cultural differences can create misunderstanding when people share feelings. Think about how you would handle each situation if you were the person in the example.

Some cultures practice less expressiveness than others.

Bill and his wife Lorraine have a recurring argument. She contends, "You never tell me anything," and "You never share your feelings with me." She thinks, "What is he hiding?"

Bill on the other hand insists, "I tell you everything that I think is important and worth telling," while he thinks to himself, "Why does she seem so insecure?"

How could you better manage your spoken words and unspoken thoughts if you were Bill?

_____

_____

If you were Lorraine? _____

_____

CONTINUED

Annette, a Native American, appears very shy when other people ask her personal questions or even when they compliment her. She avoids answering them, and keeps silent. The women with whom she works see her behavior as standoffish. Annette would like to have more friends and can't understand why people aren't friendlier with her.

What would you do if you were Annette? _____

_____

If you were a woman working with Annette? _____

_____

Public displays of anger are absolutely forbidden in some cultures, whereas in others, people are free to raise their voices and use large gestures.

Marva works in the export department of a large multinational corporation. She was brought up in an "old world" family where, as she describes it, "arguing was our weekend entertainment." Her associates were raised in families where arguing was frowned upon. They back off from Marva's confrontational style and describe her as pushy.

What would you do if you were Marva? _____

_____

As one of Marva's associates? _____

_____

"Eyes are windows of the soul." Our eyes reveal the feelings, attitudes, and relationships of people to each other, but "eye language" may differ from one culture to another. The following example is from "Black Boss, White Boss," from ODT Inc. Look at the confusion that different eye signals give:

Charles, who is white, is speaking to his employer John, who is black. John rarely looks at Charles and Charles is wondering if John is actually listening to him. When it's John's turn to speak, he looks steadily at Charles and Charles looks back at him. Both begin to feel like the other is being rude or even aggressive. They close the meeting uneasily and walk away with a feeling of dislike for each other.

Some, especially working class black people tend to look almost steadily at the listener while talking, but when listening tend to make only occasional eye contact. Western European and U.S. whites, as listeners, tend to look steadily at the speaker, but when speaking themselves make eye contact less frequently.

If I were Charles I might: _____

_____

As John I might: _____

_____

Compare your answers with the author's suggested responses in the back of the book.

Match Your Partner's Unspoken Behavior

Did you ever notice how you sometimes unconsciously copy what another person does? They fold their arms; you fold yours. They cross their legs; you cross yours, and so forth. Imitation is normal when growing up. You can see it when children play "grown-up." Even as adults we often automatically tend to imitate others to become comfortable with them or to feel at home in a new culture.

Learning by imitation is a slow process. However, we may also consciously improve our rapport with another person by matching or mirroring:

- ➤ **Tone of voice-high or low**–pitch, musicality.

- ➤ **Body posture**–position of arms, legs, body forward, and so on.

- ➤ **Breathing rate**–fast or slow, tense or relaxed.

- ➤ **Comfortable distance**–the distance that feels comfortable for the other person; remain within the range they set.

- ➤ **Timing and pacing of speech patterns**–fast, slow, length of pauses between words, sentences, or the time it takes to begin to speak after the other has spoken, and so on.

Practice

Take the opportunity to meet someone from another culture at lunch or in some informal setting. At various points in the conversation match the nonverbal actions of the person. Be careful not to exaggerate or call attention to your attempts to match their behavior. Also, even though you are matching tone of voice and pacing, do not try to imitate another person's accent.

Observe how you feel and how the other person reacts. Do not try to match everything at once—practice with one thing at a time and do it for short periods of time only. Note any interesting outcomes below.

_____

_____

_____

Talk Sense

How we use our senses shapes how we think and determines what we are likely to pay attention to. We remember and think about things as we saw, heard, or felt them. Most individuals and cultures prefer some senses over others, though all cultures use all of the senses at one time or another.

 Some people are visual. They prefer to think with their mind's eye. They prefer words that enable them to picture and see things. They value what they see over what they hear.

 Others think in words that help them hear things. These are auditory thinkers. They prefer being told about things rather than reading about them, for example.

 Still others imagine things in terms of movement, feeling, and action. Albert Einstein used this kinesthetic type of thinking when he formulated his famous theory of relativity. These thinkers take their cues on how to act from how a situation "feels" to them.

CASE STUDY: Thinking Styles

The following story illustrates how senses shape our thinking:

Three friends went sailing together for the first time. That evening George, the boat's captain, took them to dinner and asked each of his friends how they enjoyed the trip. Walt told how he enjoyed the sounds of the waves slapping against the bow and the singing of the wind through the rigging. Marianne remembered how the rocking motion of the boat relaxed her to the point where she took a nap in the warm sun on the deck. Nico described the magnificent color contrast between the white sails and the blue sky.

What is the preferred thinking style (visual, auditory, kinesthetic) of:

Walt? _____

Marianne? _____

Nico? _____

George? _____

Compare your answers with the author's responses in the back of the book.

Getting and Using Verbal Clues

The words people use also give us clues about how they like to think. You can build better rapport with people by using words that match their thinking style. This will help them understand you better as well as increase their comfort and trust. To do this, look for verbal clues to how they think. For example:

If their verbal clue is . . .	Your response could be . . .
Give me the big picture.	*Here's how it looks. Imagine . . .*
That doesn't sound right to me	*Well, then, listen to this . . .*
The objectives feel appropriate	*Let me touch on the timetable.*

Practice

Imagine someone has asked you these questions. How might you answer?

What's the outlook? _____

_____

_____

_____

What do you hear about Jill? _____

_____

_____

_____

Do you have a grasp of what it means? _____

_____

_____

_____

Sexual Orientation

What do these famous people have in common?

Roberta Achtenberg–Former U.S. Assistant Secretary for Fair Housing and Equal Opportunity

James Baldwin–Author, civil rights activist

David Geffen–Entertainment industry mogul

Allen Ginsberg–Writer and poet

Michelangelo–Renaissance painter, sculptor, architect, and inventor

Martina Navratilova–Seven-time Wimbledon Tennis Champion

Eleanor Roosevelt–U.S. First Lady 1932–1945, advocate of the poor

Bessie Smith–Blues singer

They all are famous gay, lesbian, or bisexual people.

Of course, not all gay people are distinguished or famous. So let's get the important facts clear:

➤ Gays and lesbians are estimated to comprise between 6 and 12% of the general population.

➤ Gay people are diverse. They are found in every race, ethnic group, generation, profession, and social class.

➤ Although some gays have cultivated distinctive styles of living and behavior, you can't tell who is gay or not with any certainty simply by observing them.

➤ Gays are no more sexually aggressive than the general population.

➤ AIDS is not a specifically gay disease. More hetero- and bisexual people suffer from AIDS than do homosexuals.

*For more information, read *Sexual Orientation in the Workplace* by Amy J. Zuckerman and George F. Simons, Sage Publications.

A MATCHING GAME: HOW DO WE TALK ABOUT IT?

Many people find it very hard to talk about sexual orientation. Knowing the correct terms helps reduce the fear of embarrassment. Match each term with its correct definition by connecting them with a line.

1. Bisexual

    A. A woman who is attracted to women.

2. Gay

    B. A man who loves men. Also an umbrella term for all homosexuals.

3. Heterosexual

    C. A person who is attracted to members of the same sex.

4. Homosexual

    D. A person who has an intimate relationship and lives with another person of either sex without being married.

5. Lesbian

    E. A person who is attracted to members of the opposite sex.

6. Straight

    F. Another word for heterosexual.

7. Domestic Partner

    G. A person who is attracted to members of either sex.

Other terms like fag, dyke, queen, butch, femme, queer, and so on, while they may be used as in-group talk by some gay people, are not appropriate in the workplace. Sexual orientation is usually preferred to sexual preference, because it conveys the fact that many people feel they are gay by nature, not simply by choice.

Remember, here as elsewhere, the best way to talk about groups of people is by using the names which they prefer to be called.

Compare your answers to the author's responses in the back of the book.

Our Toughest Challenge

In recent years, more hate crimes and violence have been directed toward gay, lesbian, and bisexual people than against any other group. At work they are often an invisible, abused, and unprotected group. Consultant Dr. Ellen Abell, writing in *Managing Diversity,* suggests seven ways to include such employees fully in organizational life. You can use the following as a "can do" list to check your behavior and your organization's policies.

Can I or my organization:

➤ **Not assume everyone is heterosexual?** Since such a large part of the population is lesbian or gay, it is very likely that gays and lesbians have been working beside me as respected friends and colleagues for most of my working life.

➤ **Avoid language that excludes?** Does the wording on memos, job applications, and in conversation include lesbian and gay employees? For example, does the invitation to the shop or office party say "spouses," or use open language like "partners," "friends" or "significant others"? Or, does it assume that everyone is married, regardless of his or her sexual orientation?

➤ **Provide policies and benefits that honor different lifestyles and relationships?** Has your organization added "sexual orientation" to its antidiscrimination policy? If so, are all members of the organization aware of this and what it means? Are domestic partners covered by health insurance and other benefits packages?

➤ **Include sexual orientation in diversity programming?** Does diversity training reduce the risk of physical danger, fear, low morale, and job loss that lesbians, gays, and bisexuals may experience as a result of discomfort and ignorance on the part of others?

➤ **Look at existing attitudes and assumptions?** Most of us want to be fair and treat others equally, yet we all have biases and sometimes feel uncomfortable. This keeps us from realizing our full potential. Have I sorted out how I am going to work with someone of a different sexual orientation?

➤ **Ask lesbians, gays, and bisexuals about their lives?** The best way to learn about others is to ask them about themselves. Most people welcome genuine interest, and gay people are no exception.

➤ **Be an ally?** Can I draw on my own experiences with prejudice and unfairness to understand and support gay people in my workplace? Can I speak up when others are insensitive or unfair in what they do or say?

Americans with Disabilities

In the United States, the Americans with Disabilities Act of 1990 (ADA), provides strong legal support for making sure that this large and valuable group of people can make their full contribution to the workplace and the economy.

Disabled individuals are those with physical or mental impairments that substantially limit a major life activity (for example, hearing, seeing, speaking, breathing, learning, manual tasks, walking). The law covers persons who have a record of such impairments, as well as cancer. Also protected by ADA are those mistakenly regarded as having a disability, for example, someone who is assumed to be HIV-positive.

The ADA guarantees that disabled persons qualified to perform the essential functions of a job, with or without reasonable accommodation, will not be discriminated against in hiring and promotion in most public and private organizations. Most of the accommodations made by employers are simple modifications to workspace, or devices that enable disabled people to perform their tasks or do them more effectively, and which cost less than $50.00. If you don't know what people with disabilities need to do their job better, ask them.

Going Beyond the Law

While complying with the law goes a long way toward insuring fairness and opportunity, managing our minds to see persons with disabilities in a new light is a much bigger task. Most people who have never experienced a disability have no idea how attitudes, behaviors, and words, even well-intended ones, can be or feel damaging.

---

*For more information on ADA, read *Americans with Disabilities Act,* by Mary B. Dickson, Crisp Publications.

Here are some personal and cultural objectives that will help us go beyond the law in making our workplace friendly for people with disabilities. Below each of the following paragraphs, list one thing that you personally could do to help achieve the objective. Discuss your actions with others.

1. **See people with disabilities as people, not as oddities.** In the past, people viewed bodily disfigurement and disabilities as a sign of moral or psychological evil. We need to see people with disabilities as normal human beings with typical everyday problems and triumphs. Many disabled people have struggled to overcome great odds to be where they are. For most, however, the hardest and most abnormal part of their lives is living with the ignorance and prejudices of others.

   _____

   _____

2. **Manage your words.** Many of us need to rein in some of the words we use to talk about people with disabilities. "What are you, deaf?" "Are you blind?" These comments are not respectful. However, seeing disabilities in a new light does not automatically give us a new set of words to use. We will probably have quite a few laughs and maybe some embarrassing moments while we try to create them.

   _____

   _____

3. **Face your own fears instead of projecting them onto others.** Seeing others' disabilities can remind us that we are fragile and vulnerable. Sometimes we would rather not look at this side of life. Having to deal with a person with a disability at work challenges us to confront our fears and stereotypes. You have a chance to grow emotionally and spiritually as you strive to work smoothly with this person.

   _____

   _____

4. **Resist the temptation to overly care for people with disabilities.** They want to face challenges and be in charge of their lives as much as anyone else. Doing too much can feel patronizing and annoying to them. For many this just hurts their self-esteem. Everyone needs some help at one time or another, but if you're unsure, just ask.

   _____

   _____

5. **See accommodations as a normal part of making things work on the job.** Everyone needs things that make his or her job easier, more effective, and more pleasant, but we tend to notice such things more when people have disabilities. You may have brought a cushion to work to sit on to reach your keyboard more comfortably, or got the boss to improve the lighting. Accommodating co-workers with disabilities is the same thing—another normal part of working together.

   _____

   _____

6. **Be sensitive to the range of challenges that come with different kinds of disabilities.** Although the wheelchair is used as an international symbol of disability, many disabilities are not visible. Being sensitive and alert to people's perceived disabilities, whether they fully fit the legal definition of disabled or not, is simply good business practice. People have unseen sensitivities, allergies, and addictions, as well as temporary or life-threatening illnesses. Some may have mental or emotional disabilities.

   _____

   _____

Beauty in the Workplace

People with visible disabilities easily become targets of society's discomfort with those who are not seen as "whole and wholesome." Unfortunately, prejudice and fear do not end with disabilities. Hiring, firing, promotions, and other workplace decisions are too often made on the basis of likes and dislikes about how others look. Despite the message of advertising, a happy society and a productive workplace cannot value only those who are lighter skinned, thinner, younger, or cuter.

We have already seen how the mind automatically judges what it sees as good and beautiful versus what is bad and ugly. We can't stop ourselves from thinking, but we can work to change how we judge what is beautiful or ugly. Some places in the United States have tried to create laws against "looks-ism," that is, discriminating against people on the basis of how they look. Just what looks-ism involves, however, is very hard to define and enforce. Organizations have the right to set dress codes that are appropriate for their businesses as well as to enforce workplace standards of health and cleanliness, but the issue here is the unfairness that results from our unconscious reactions to others simply because of how they look to us.

Practice

Take two or three minutes to think about someone you know or work with who might not be considered beautiful or handsome by popular cultural standards (that includes almost all of us). Below, make a list of the things about that person that you feel expresses his or her true worth or beauty. Then do the same thing for yourself.

Another's true worth or beauty:

_____

_____

_____

_____

_____

My true worth or beauty:

_____

_____

_____

_____

_____

P A R T 4

Taking Action

Two Sides of Diversity

When working in your own culture, it is normal to think of your reality as everybody's reality—as "how things are supposed to be"—and expect everyone else to fit in, since you feel you know best. When you are in somebody else's culture, things are different. You are the one who's out of sync. You may feel shy, wrong, guilty, stupid, or ashamed, even though you are doing your best to understand and work with others. Here is an example of something that often happens when women work in a strongly male culture.

Jack considers himself a fair, honest, and hard-working manager. He regularly chairs a meeting with three other managers, only one of whom, Marcia, is a woman. Marcia and Jack enjoy each other's company when they work together.

One day, Marcia came to Jack, angry to the point of tears, and complained bitterly. "At this morning's meeting, Jack," she said, "I was the first person to give a solution to our sales problem. You interrupted at the end of my presentation to let Dwight speak. A half-hour later when we finally adopted my approach, you gave Dwight credit for it!" While saying this to Jack, Marcia is saying to herself, "What's wrong with me, that nobody listens?"

Jack is bewildered. He doesn't remember interrupting Marcia. Now, only because she mentioned it, does he recall that she said something about the idea early in the meeting. He wonders what's wrong with Marcia today, "Why is she making such a big deal out of what happened?" He tries to make light of the situation so Marcia will feel better.

This is not surprising. Walter LeFlore, an organizational systems consultant, wisely observed, "that which is seen as 'different' is treated as if it were 'less than' that which is generally seen as being normal." In other words, different usually means inferior.

CASE STUDY: Culture Shock

When we work or live in someone else's culture, we go through culture shock. People respond to culture shock in three ways. Most of us do some of each. Look at the descriptions and examples below and list any ways in which you may have acted like the people in each example.

People are exhibiting culture shock when they:

1. **Reject the culture they are in and stick to their own.** People who persist in this rarely learn to live and work with people in the new culture successfully. They think they are right and everyone else wrong.

   Peggy is one of few women in an engineering firm. She dislikes the men she works with, and sees them as "typical" of the culture of men. Men, as she sees it, cause wars, economic disasters, and domestic violence. In short, they are responsible for all that's wrong with the world. Any failure on her part she views as the result of male dominance.

   When I am not a member of the prevailing culture, here are ways I reject (or consider rejecting) others as Peggy does:

   _____

   _____

2. **"Go native," trying to be more native than the natives themselves. This is usually done at the expense of one's self-esteem.**

   Jon Marks (he changed his name from Juan Marcos) is trying desperately to succeed in sales. He had his hair lightened and wears "preppy" fashions. He hates going home to his family. They remind him of all that's backward in his native country. It's hard for him to say no, so he always promises more than he can deliver. He doesn't feel good about himself and rarely tells the truth when people ask personal questions.

Ways I "go native" as Jon does, when I try to succeed in someone else's culture:

_____

_____

3. **Adapt.** People value themselves and their culture but also strive to understand the culture they are in and learn the skills they need to become more effective. They concentrate on what works and what is fair rather than who's right or wrong.

   Lamar works hard to hold down his first job out of school. He realizes that some people are uncomfortable around him because he is black, but he's found others in the firm who will support him and help him to succeed. Right now he is working hard to learn the large number of technical terms used in his new business, as well as the jargon used around the office.

   Ways I adapt as Lamar does, respecting myself and doing what works and is fair to others:

_____

_____

Culture–Living, Growing, Changing

Culture is alive and changing, always evolving into something new and different. No one can entirely protect his or her culture from change. If you are in the prevailing culture, you are likely to think of your way of doing things as the norm, at least unconsciously. It may be hard for you to see how your point of view can distort and even damage how you see other cultures. Ask others how your culture influences theirs. You could be in for an enlightening and possibly upsetting conversation. Consider the following example:

Theo works for a large manufacturer of compact discs and tapes in the Netherlands. At an international business meeting, he is at lunch with Pak Tirta, a Sumatran businessman. Theo loudly berates the backwardness of the Indonesian government on importing electronic media. Pak Tirta is amiable but says very little. Inwardly he is embarrassed and offended. Pak Tirta thinks Theo is a perfect example of why one must be cautious about letting certain Western influences into his country. Theo leaves the table feeling satisfied, thinking that this smiling Indonesian is a good sign that things may be changing.

All of us, whether in the prevailing culture or not, face a wholesale attack on our inherited cultural values by the widespread influence of the media. This is not to accuse the media of evil intentions, even though deliberate propaganda campaigns sometimes occur. It is simply to say that media influences are powerful and hard to resist.

The messages of radio, television, video, and audio recordings can drown out the voices of tradition and the efforts of parents and teachers to teach their children other values. The difference between reality and entertainment is easily blurred.

It is not surprising that curbs are placed on the use of media by individuals, families, and governments in many parts of the world. Such curbs range from regulating computer trading on the stock exchange, where machines actually make decisions, to banning the importation of rock music, as well as other forms of censorship.

YOUR POWER OVER THE MEDIA

What should you do if these powerful forces threaten your culture? There are no easy answers but here are some partial ones. Check (✔) the ones that you feel you can do:

❏ I am alert and aware of what is taking place in the media and how it affects my cultural values.

❏ I patronize and use media that support the values I profess.

❏ I let my feelings and values be known, especially when something in the media offends me or my culture. I support positive and multicultural programming.

❏ I am active in the media. I encourage involvement in positive programming.

❏ I find ways of using the media to support important values of my culture and to learn about the cultures of others.

Culture Shift

Until recently, trade, industry, and business in the United States has been largely conducted by white men. However, the U.S. Department of Labor statistics and other projections show that:

➤ White men are now less than half of the U.S. workforce.

➤ Foreign-owned companies employ about 4% of the U.S. workforce. In the chemical industry about half of U.S. workers are working for foreign-owned companies.

➤ By 2025, only 9% of those entering the U.S. workforce will be white men, 42% will be white women, and the balance will be made up of African-Americans and immigrants. Nearly a third of the new entrants will be men and women of color.

➤ Immigrants will represent the largest share of the increase of the U.S. population and workforce.

Statistics may not be perfectly accurate, but they do show trends. Other surprising statistics could be cited for the shifts of population and culture in nations around the world. You can see it in the faces of the people on the streets of major cities. Dr. Lucia Edmonds and Jimmy Jones, experts in multicultural development, have observed:

"Corporations and organizations that do not work assertively with multiculturalism will ultimately do poorly in the world marketplace. They will face workplace disharmony, balkanization of the work force, greater labor-management tensions, higher discrimination case costs, loss of domestic and international markets, and loss of productivity."

Time Out

Congratulate yourself for having the interest and commitment to pick up this book and work through it this far! Personally and professionally you are learning the skills to succeed in a multicultural world. But, how is your workplace or organization doing? Below is the ladder that most organizations have to climb to deal successfully with cultural diversity. Look at the ladder from the bottom up and check (✔) the level that you feel your organization or your part of it has reached. Discuss your rating with others to find out what they think.

When it comes to cultural change and multicultural awareness, here is where my organization stands on the ladder to success:

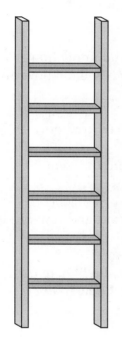

We are benefiting from using the talents of a multicultural workforce.

There is an overall plan and concentrated effort.

Disconnected efforts are taking place.

We have decided that changes have to be made.

We have created an open forum for discussion.

There is anger and frustration over diversity.

People actively deny that diversity could be important to deal with.

There are problems, but no one is aware that diversity is an issue.

What steps do you feel should be taken next?

1. _____

2. _____

Who will you make aware of them?

_____

How to Deal with the Prevailing Culture

Depending on where we find ourselves, we may sometimes be part of a prevailing or insider culture and at other times be an outsider. Use the two checklists below to create your own personal plan for improving multicultural harmony and collaboration. The first checklist is for those who see themselves as part of the prevailing culture; the second is for those outside it.

Check (✔) the items that are true of you.

Hint: The more true answers the better! However, don't kid yourself about your performance in these areas. Get feedback from others.

1. When I belong to the prevailing culture:

❑ I am aware that I am part of a prevailing culture and know how it works. I listen to people of other cultures when they tell me how my culture affects them.

❑ I am committed to fairness and I let others in my culture know it.

❑ I look to people of other cultures for fresh ideas and different perspectives on my life.

❑ I make sure that members of other cultures are heard and respected for their differences.

❑ I coach outsiders on how to succeed in my culture. I tell them the unwritten rules and show them what they need to know to operate better.

❑ I make sure that my subordinates and colleagues from other cultures are prepared for what they have to do to meet the demands of my culture.

❑ When I train or coach outsiders, I do not put them down or undermine the value of their differences.

❑ I give outsiders my personal support and loyalty even if they are rejected or criticized by members of my own culture.

❑ I am aware that outsiders often see how my culture works better than I do, and I go to them to learn about the effect of things that I do and say.

❑ I recognize that if I am under pressure I tend to make myself and my culture right and others wrong.

❑ I apologize when I have done something to offend someone of another background.

❑ In the workplace, when accountable to someone of a different culture, I avoid the tendency to go over his or her head to a person of my own culture.

❑ I make outsiders aware of unfair traditions, rules, and ways of behaving in my culture or organization and work with them to change things.

❑ I resist the temptation to make another group the scapegoat when something goes wrong.

❑ I am not afraid to give those from other cultures honest, helpful, and sensitive feedback about how they perform on the job.

❑ I distribute information to whomever should get it, regardless of cultural differences.

❑ I go out of my way to recruit, select, train, and promote capable people from outside the prevailing culture.

2. When I belong to an "outsider" culture:

❑ I realize that, because of my background, I have something special to contribute to my organization.

❑ Even when rejected, I take pride in my culture. I take steps to build my self-esteem and the self-esteem of others who, like me, do not belong to the prevailing culture.

❑ While I do not have to give up my own culture to fit in, I realize that I may have to learn new information and practice new skills to succeed.

❏ I look for members of the prevailing culture who will help me read between the lines to understand the unwritten rules about how the system works.

❏ When I succeed in the prevailing culture, I am careful not to think of myself as an exception or separate myself from others of my background.

❏ I share what I learn about the insider culture with others like myself.

❏ I am careful under pressure not to automatically make myself and my culture right and others wrong.

❏ I sympathize and work with other outsider groups to achieve common objectives in the prevailing culture.

❏ I resist the tendency to cluster only with my own kind or only with people from the insider culture when I am in mixed company.

❏ I resist blaming the insider group for everything that goes wrong.

❏ I share with members of the prevailing culture the special qualities and achievements of my own culture.

❏ I know how to present differing points of view in ways that others can hear and understand.

❏ I can respect individuals of other cultures and treat them fairly and with respect even though I may be fiercely committed to conflicting political goals.

❏ I know how to refresh myself from the wellsprings of my own culture when I am tired out by my efforts to understand and work in the prevailing culture.

P A R T 5

Diversity and Globalization

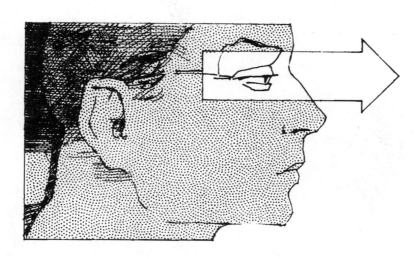

What Is Globalization?

Globalization refers to the increasingly worldwide movement of people, goods, products, and services. It is not a new phenomenon, but one that has made great strides in recent years because of the power that information technology, the Internet, and the news and entertainment media to create worldwide communication networks.

Globalization results from our ability to create large economic systems, worldwide banking, and open trade areas like NAFTA and the European Community. Companies compete to create global brands and vie with each other in a global talent pool to find the best and the brightest people, wherever their place of origin. Even terrorism, as we have sadly learned, has become globalized.

Globalization has positive and negative sides, opportunities and threats, supporters and protesters. It offers us new challenges to manage our minds, words, and actions amid the shifting relationships, the stresses and strains that arise between the world's nations, cultures, and regions. We face the ethical and economic challenges of creating a sustainable planet in which people can share resources, conduct good business, and live in peace.

The increase in mobility, instant worldwide communication, and our need to work across old borders and boundaries mean even more diversity than ever before. What does globalization mean to you? How do you manage your mind when things are changing so rapidly? What are your hopes and fears about an even more diverse future? What opportunities and threats do you see in dealing with more kinds of people around the world?

Hopes and Opportunities	Threats and Fears

The New Workplace Is Everywhere

Most business today is being changed by information technology. We need new skills and new ways of working to succeed in this shifting environment.

New ways of working do not make our cultural tendencies disappear; but they often make diversity harder to recognize and manage. To see how differences affect us when working together online or virtually, imagine a wheel.

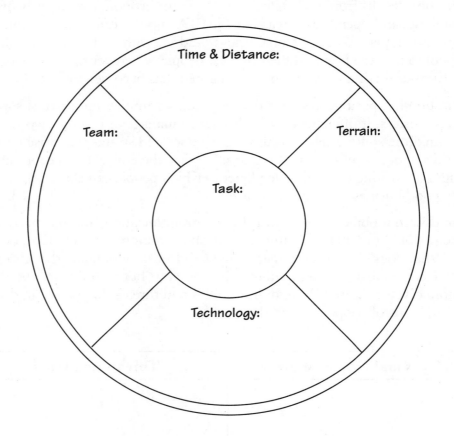

In the center of the wheel is an axle, the **task** or job that virtual workers or teams do to help the organization reach its goals. Culture can be the "grit" that slows down or keeps the wheel from running smoothly, or it can be the "grease" that lets the wheel roll faster and smoother. It depends on how you manage it! Think of your virtual work with people who are different from you, and make notes on the wheel itself about things you want to manage or discuss with your virtual co-workers or team. On the following page are the areas you'll want to consider.

Task How does culture and background affect how you and others see your task? How could these different views of the task be shared and used to do a better job or create a better product or service? Note this in the center of the wheel.

Surrounding the task are four challenges that must be dealt with successfully if your virtual cooperation is to roll along smoothly and in balance. They are:

Time & Distance Differing ideas and expectations about how time should be used, and the absence of face-to-face contact can quickly cause breakdowns in communication, authority, and commitments. How do time zones and distance affect the ways in which you communicate and manage people and projects across widespread locations and cultures? How does the way that different people value time, use time, or react to distance cause misunderstanding or conflict? What ground rules could you create together that would help you work better? Put your ideas in the time and distance part of the wheel.

Terrain The organizational settings we work in may differ in various places. Are there different styles and levels of management support and differing approaches to decision-making and delegation where you and your virtual co-workers do your job? What could you or your team do to better communicate your new ways of working, so that your efforts at working together across cultures are seen, understood, and acknowledged? Make notes on this in the terrain section of the wheel.

Technology Some people prefer email to phone conferences, frequent meetings to teleconferences, and so on. Some are enthusiastic and some are afraid of technology. How do you choose the right virtual tools and learn to work with them effectively across cultures? How can you use your virtual tools to do the team's assigned business task as well as keep team spirit up? Write what you think in the technology part of the wheel.

Team Multicultural teamwork is hard enough in face-to-face teams. It demands even more attention when we work virtually. How do people from different cultures understand teamwork, individual initiative, and their responsibility to each other when working virtually? How do social expectations of a team differ? How can you resolve these differences or use them to make the team work together even better? Put your ideas in the team part of the wheel.

Managing Your Words

For the first time in world history, there are more people who speak a language, English, as a second language than there are native-born speakers of that language. Surprisingly these speakers of English as a second language (ESL) often understand each other better than they do the people who speak English as their mother tongue because they use simpler words and grammar when speaking with each other.

When using English in a multicultural environment, work at expressing yourself in simple and clear terms. The Canadian Government provides an online course called "Plain Train" which is found at http://www.plainlanguagenetwork.org/plaintrain/ that can help you learn to speak and write more simply and clearly. Here are some examples they give of how you can be better understood by avoiding jargon and difficult words and phrases, and choosing easy-to-understand terms:

INSTEAD OF...	USE...
accomplish	do
ascertain	find out
disseminate	send out, distribute
endeavor	try
expedite	hasten, speed up
facilitate	make easier, help
formulate	work out, devise, form
in lieu of	instead of
locality	place
optimum	best, greatest, most
strategize	plan
utilize	use

Practice

What other things can we do to help ourselves better understand each other?

As a native language speaker:

1. _____

2. _____

3. _____

As a person who must work in a second language:

1. _____

2. _____

3. _____

People on the Move

The economic opportunities of globalization, as well as forces like political and religious persecution, war, and natural disasters cause many people to find or seek a new home or a place to work far away from the land of their origins. Worldwide, more people are moving than ever before. Perhaps you live or work with such people. Perhaps you yourself or one or both of your parents moved here. Understanding the challenges and problems that come with these shifts is a good way to help yourself and others feel more comfortable and become more productive at work.

Depending on the economic and political situation, at any given time countries may welcome or resist the arrival of people from other places. Part of working together successfully may require us to come to grips with our attitudes about the movement of people in the world and more specifically, those around us.

Practice

Think for a moment. What are the feelings of people you know and work with? How do they describe and discuss people who have arrived from elsewhere? What might you like to change about this? Make some notes about this that you might want to discuss with others.

_____

_____

_____

_____

_____

WHO ARE THESE NEW PEOPLE?

Below are 10 terms used to describe different people and the conditions or reasons for their moving from one place to another. In some cases more than one term may apply to the same person. See if you can match the terms on the left with their meanings.

Name

_____ Asylum seeker

_____ Displaced person

_____ Economic refugee

_____ Emigrant

_____ Émigré

_____ Expatriate

_____ Immigrant

_____ Migrant

_____ Refugee

_____ Virtual expatriate

Description

A. A person who leaves his or her native country to live and work elsewhere

B. A person who moves regularly in order to find work

C. A person who flees to a foreign country to escape danger or persecution

D. A person who comes to a country to take up permanent residence

E. Someone fleeing from a place where poverty is endemic or where there is less opportunity, in order to seek better opportunities elsewhere

F. A person forced to emigrate for political reasons

G. A person who is departing or has departed from a country to settle elsewhere

H. Someone expelled or forced to flee from home or homeland

I. A person who by technology does his or her work in another country

J. A person who flees to another country to seek protection from arrest or persecution in his or her own country

Compare your answers with the author's suggested responses in the back of the book.

Managing Your Actions in the Face of Global Stress

As we noted earlier, when we are under stress, we tend to revert to our basic identity. We become more patriotic, more religious, and more defensive of ourselves and our families. We start playing old roles. We wave more flags. We become more Latino or more Anglo, more macho or more fundamentalist. We tend to unite with people like us against people who are different from us. Why? Because stress makes us think and feel that we need to preserve ourselves against the outside forces that cause us stress.

This is a natural and normal response to threat. This is true whether the threat is very real or only seen as real. Sometimes it is hard to know the difference!

It is precisely at such stressful times that we need to keep our awareness of diversity and our values of fairness in focus. So what can we do? On the next page, you will find a number of steps to take. Use them as a checklist when global events, organizational change, or conflicts of diversity are making their effects strongly felt where you work or where you live.

Improving Your Reactions to Stress

Gauge your ability to manage each step and to see if you need to get help from others. Use the stressful situation as an opportunity to put diversity to work for you by talking to and working with people who are different from you. Perhaps together you can manage or change the stressful situation.

Easy for me	Can do	Need Help	
			I can talk about my feelings both to people like me and to people different from me.
			I can accept my emotions and manage to keep them from turning into rash or hurtful acts.
			I can listen to others who are expressing strong or even negative feelings, and empathize, even though I may not agree with them.
			I can research the facts about a situation and separate them from rhetoric and propaganda.
			I can avoid lumping people into groups and not lose sight of their many differences.
			I can avoid blaming groups of people for the actions of individuals.
			I can keep from being "swept away by the crowd."
			I can stay curious and educate myself about others' differences, for example, learn about their values, beliefs, and history, even when we appear to be in conflict.
			I can exercise tolerance as well as ask or expect it of others.
			I know how to clarify my values and express them to others without being aggressive.
			I can join with others in promoting points of view and proposing solutions without losing my ability to see value in the perspectives of those who oppose us.

Conclusion

Diversity Asks Something of Everyone

Diversity is the sum total of the resources (values, habits, skills, knowledge, customs, and so on) that can be found in a multicultural group. Diversity gives a group of people more possibilities and opportunities, if they learn how to recognize and use it. The success of organizations and communities depends on our ability to use diversity in productive and creative ways rather than being bound up in fears, resentments, and prejudices. How do we do this?

Working across cultures forces us to look at what we assume about the task at hand. This means talking to each other about what we want, how we think we should go about getting it, and, at every step, taking nothing for granted.

Perhaps because the United States has long been diverse, it has developed a culture in which people are very direct in speaking with each other and asking questions. Newcomers from less diverse backgrounds may find themselves embarrassed by such directness and hesitate to offend others with their questions.

Being explicit, however hard, is a skill that we all have to develop in the face of our differences. According to Lisa Adent Hoecklin*, successful cultural learning and creativity in a multicultural group occurs when we take four critical steps.

- ➤ Make our cultural assumptions explicit, that is, establish a respectful process by which we regularly examine and share what lies behind our thinking. This demands that we listen and ask questions.

- ➤ Agree on what we are trying to do or create together when we set out on a project or start a discussion.

- ➤ Examine the reasons why each culture approaches the task, topic, or objective as it does. We use this information to decide whose way or what combination of ways will create what we want.

- ➤ Examine our results and how we got to them so we can improve them and work together even better the next time.

---

* Lisa Adent Hoecklin, *Managing Cultural Differences for Competition Advantage,* The Economist Intelligence Unit. We have modified Ms. Hoecklin's decision tree model to broaden its applicability.

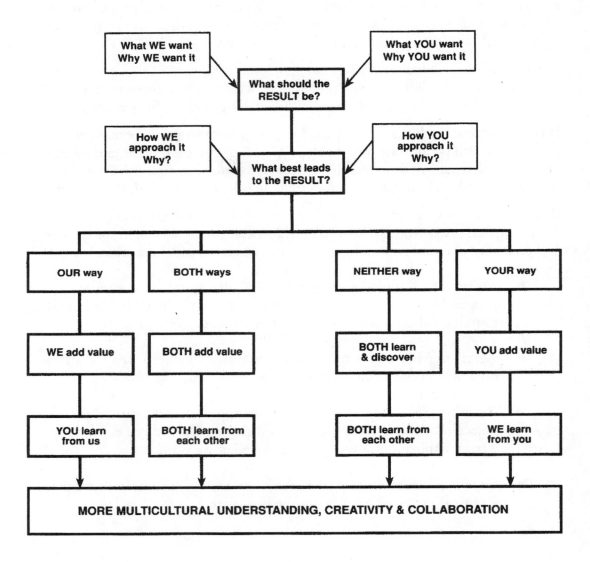

The Steps We Take to Work Together

Put in the form of a decision tree, working together looks like this:

What Next?

1. Get information about others.

You can learn about the cultures of other people in many ways. You can read books and articles, visit the Internet, see films and videos, and join e-learning programs about other cultures. At the end of this section there is a list of resources that will reinforce what you have learned and help you learn more.

Still, what you learn in books or videos only hints at what other people actually experience. They alert you to particular ways in which others might be different from you. You need to get to know people, not just about them.

Traveling or living abroad, spending time in other people's homes or neighborhoods can bring you closer to other cultures. Most of us, particularly if we belong to a prevailing culture, are like tourists in other people's cultures. We have a lot to learn and we should be polite and very slow to judge what we see.

2. Respect individual differences.

Neither you nor anybody else can make general statements that are valid about another person based only on what you know about his or her culture. However, knowing what people value, their customs and ideas, will give you helpful clues when working with someone whose culture is different from yours.

Remember the cake on page 5. There are many things that may make one person different from another even when they belong to the same culture. Assuming that a person is the way he or she is only because of personality traits or because of race or religion is unfair. Everyone is unique with many dimensions. We need to pay attention to the whole person.

Daniel and Andy are both from the Philippines. They came together to work in California. Daniel is exuberant and flowery in the way he speaks. Even though his work is solid, it took a long time for his US colleagues to trust him. They thought he was exaggerating or covering up something. Andy, on the other hand, is quiet and does not speak until spoken to. Even though he does superior work, people read him as being unsociable and not a good team worker. His manager even sent him off to a communications course to improve his listening skills, when in fact, he already was an excellent listener.

If we take into allowance:

The Individual

+

Personal History

+

Cultural Background

+

The Situation

We start to reach   →   The Whole Person

3. Be curious and ask questions.

The best information comes straight from people themselves. Be friendly and curious, respectful and slow to judge others.

Here are some ways to ask questions when you want to know how others think:

What does it mean to you when . . .?

What do you say to yourself about . . .?

What's it like for you when . . .?

What do you imagine when you say . . .?

How do you picture it?

Tell me what is important to you.

Show me how you would do . . .

How would you express or describe . . .?

How important for you is . . .?

What concerns do you have about . . .?

4. Understand your own culture.

Seeing yourself as a product of one among many cultures, especially if your culture is the prevailing one, is critically important if you are to understand how other people relate to you.

When studying others' cultures you will discover things about them that they don't know about themselves. But most importantly you will become aware of what is different and special about your background. Not only can you communicate and work better together, but you can learn new and interesting ways to do things and look at things. People who are different can bring out the best in us if we let them.

Sometimes, there can be real conflicts between values we are unwilling to change or give up. This is when we need to learn to respect each other as well as agree to disagree. When you discover something about another person's culture that you can't accept, try not to reject or blame the person. Find new ways to deal with behaviors that frustrate or irritate you. Blame leads to anger, prejudice, and unfairness.

This book was written to bring fresh ideas and new ways of behaving into your life. We hope it has helped you improve how you manage your mind, how you manage your words, and how you manage the unspoken actions of your life, so you can understand others better and treat them more fairly. Read it again in a few months and rework the exercises. You can refresh your skills and see how much better you have become at managing diversity in your life and in your work.

Now, read and complete the practice exercise in the "Learning to Value Our Differences" section on the next page. It is the most important exercise of all.

Learning to Value Our Differences

We need confidence and commitment to accept, respect, and work with others successfully. Some of us have inherited or embraced religious or philosophical beliefs that make this task easier. We learned that we should "love our neighbors as ourselves," or that "all are created equal," or to "have compassion for all living beings" or "live and let live." Such values are often stated in the creeds of our faiths and in the constitutions and anthems of nations. We recite them or sing them on public occasions to remind ourselves of our basic commitments to each other.

Rather than simply paying lip service to our beliefs or values, we can really bring them to life if we:

➤ Create a clear vision of what we would like to see

➤ Commit ourselves to living it out

➤ Freely and openly tell others about it

Practice

What are your best beliefs and values about the human beings with whom you share life and work in this world, in your nation, your work place, your neighborhood? How would you picture a healthy, fair, and happy multicultural society?

I believe: _____

_____

_____

_____

I can see: _____

_____

_____

_____

_____

As the world changes, we sometimes learn that what we used to believe no longer works, or how we understand it is "too small." For example:

For over 100 years, people pictured the United States as a "great melting pot." Immigrants who were "cooked" in the crucible of togetherness would become one in culture, language, and tradition. It didn't happen that way, and fresh waves of newcomers still bring unfamiliar words and ways. Natives and earlier arrivals stubbornly and justly insist on the right to be who they are. Today the challenge for citizens of the United States is to create a new image for their future together.

When confronted in the 1950s with new waves of immigrants, Canada looked at the experience of the United States. It felt the gap that separated its English- and French-speaking citizens and the resentment that European colonization caused its first nations. It declared that it would not become a melting pot, but a great mosaic. Canada began to imagine itself as a beautiful picture created out of countless differently colored stones. Today the challenge for each Canadian is to live out this vision as he or she encounters fellow citizens of different racial and national origins.

Practice

Think about what you wrote on page 108. Compare it with what you learned in this book and to your everyday experience. Is your belief or vision in any way too small or out of date? How could you improve it? Put your answer in simple words in the space below.

_____

_____

_____

Commit yourself to improving your vision of greater cultural diversity. Pick two people with whom you will share your vision during the next week. Make a commitment to do this now.

1. _____

2. _____

Author's Notes on the Case Studies

Privacy and How We Share Feelings (pages 61–63)

Bill and Lorraine: Bill and Lorraine need to understand that men and women commonly have different expectations about sharing. Women often share to create rapport, feelings of friendship, and intimacy, while men simply report on the facts that they feel are important and feel this is the best way to support and take care of others. Not faulting each other for being different is the first step to learning more about each other's communication styles.

Annette: Creating comfortable workplace relationships is for some people a matter of making small talk, while for others small talk seems wasted time. As in so many multicultural situations, each side has to stretch a bit. Annette might find it useful to learn to make small talk, while her co-workers might learn to include Annette in their informal activities. In either case, it is again important not to judge others as wrong or false for behavior that is natural to them.

Marva: The culture of many U.S. workplaces is very resistant to conflict or what looks like conflict. This is unlikely to change much, so Marva will have to look to when it is okay and when it is not safe to be confrontational. Meanwhile her associates need to recognize that Marva may have very important and useful things to add to the conversation if they do not become emotionally resistant to the way she speaks.

Charles: Unconscious judgments and fears about racial conflict lie close to the surface for many U.S. workers. While more and more blacks and Latinos conform to white standards in workplace behavior and reserve other cultural forms of expression for home and private life, it is not uncommon for nonverbal styles to conflict as they do around eye contact in this case, leaving both parties confused. Knowing and accepting these conflicting styles in the people you commonly interact with and not judging them with your own assumptions is key. Thomas Kochman's book, *Black and White Styles in Conflict,* offers lots of information that can diffuse black-white tensions.

Thinking Styles (page 66)

Walt: auditory
Marianne: kinesthetic
Nico: visual
George: Harder to judge. His concern with taste and feeling when asking his [frie]nds about what they experienced would probably make him kinesthetic.

Author's Responses to the Exercises

Practice (page 18)

This line of characters has no message. It is a set of random symbols put here to allow you to see how your mind automatically uses its cultural "database," that is, what you already know, to interpret what it sees.

Practice (page 32)

Some tips for evaluating your choices are presented below.

1. Perhaps the best overall strategy. It shows you disapprove without disrupting what you are doing, creating a conflict, or adding more embarrassment to the situation.

2. If the humor was very offensive, or the person doesn't get the message of silence, you may want to confront the storyteller. Using the "Ouch!" technique (see page 35) is a good middle road between 1 and 2, if people know about it beforehand.

3. A poor strategy. The offender probably won't get the message, and may even interpret your behavior as a go-ahead to tell more offensive jokes.

4. Pulling the offender aside later benefits both him or her and the group insulted. Often the storyteller is ignorant or insensitive rather than malicious. Laughing, however, may encourage the storytelling to continue.

5. May lead to a fierce game of "Can you top this?" Not a good strategy in promoting understanding.

A Matching Game: How Do We Talk About It? (page 69)

1 = G, 2 = B, 3 = E, 4 = C, 5 = A, 6 = F, 7 = D

Who Are These New People? (page 97)

Name	Description
J. Asylum seeker	A person who flees to another country to seek protection from arrest or persecution in his or her own country. Such people must ask for asylum and be judged as truly oppressed, usually for political, ethnic, or religious reasons, in order to be allowed to remain in the country in which they seek protection.
H. Displaced person	Someone expelled or forced to flee from home or homeland. This older term usually refers to people deliberately and forcibly moved by governments for ethnic or political reasons. "DP" is an unfriendly word sometimes heard to describe these people.
E. Economic refugee	Someone fleeing from a place where poverty is endemic or where there is less opportunity, in order to seek better chances elsewhere. Usually arriving without permission, such persons if judged as such are often sent back to their place of origin.
G. Emigrant	A person who is departing or has departed from a country to settle elsewhere. Often confused with "immigrant," and indeed the same person, but seen from the perspective of the land he or she is leaving rather than the destination. Some parts of the world are concerned about the talent they lose because of emigration.
F. Émigré	A person forced to emigrate for political reasons. Also an older term usually used to describe in positive terms dignitaries or professionals who have fled and remained abroad.
A. Expatriate	A person who leaves his or her native country to live and work elsewhere. Expatriation is often a temporary assignment by one's organization for a specific job abroad. Despite seeking and accepting such an assignment, expatriates and their families may also face cultural challenges adapting to their new organization and life style. They need help from companies as well as from their new neighbors and colleagues to acculturate to their new environment

Name	Description
D. Immigrant	A person who comes to a country to take up permanent residence. The government classifies such people as "legal" or "illegal" depending on whether they have permission to come or not. Illegal immigrants are less protected by law and social services and are frequently taken advantage of as "cheap labor."
B. Migrant	A person who moves regularly in order to find work. Migrants may be citizens; however the term is usually used to describe those originating outside the country. They often move about as families or communities to where the work is available. Migrants often must struggle for fair wages and working conditions.
C. Refugee	A person who flees to a foreign country to escape danger or persecution. Refugees are common in times of war and when other tribal or ethnic groups threaten to oppress or eliminate them, a process known as "genocide."
I. Virtual expatriate	A person who by technology does his or her work in another country. Today many people in call centers, data processing, and a growing number of fields work from their home country, often exclusively with and for people in other countries. They are faced with the challenge of understanding how to interact with a faraway culture. They are sometimes also called "virtual immigrants" because they "emigrate" without leaving home. They are too easily seen as a function rather than as real people by those who hire them.

Resources

Sources for Diversity Information, Products, and Services

The organizations listed here are sources of products and services related to diversity.

Diversity Resources provides information and training materials on diversity in the workplace and in healthcare, and produces an annual diversity calendar. http://www.diversityresources.com/

George Simons International is a worldwide network of established professionals providing assessment, consulting, and training in the field of cultural and gender diversity and virtual global teamwork. Specializing in intercultural expertise online, they are the developers of the DIVERSOPHY® intercultural training game and a wide variety of diversity tools and instruments. http://www.diversophy.com/

The Intercultural Press Inc. provides books, simulations, and other training materials about crossing cultures for trainers, businesspeople, government representatives, educators, service organizations, travelers, expatriates, and students. http://interculturalpress.com/

The National Gay and Lesbian Task Force works to eliminate prejudice, violence, and injustice against gay, lesbian, bisexual and transgender people at the local, state, and national level and publishes a wide range of educational materials for both the homosexual and heterosexual public. http://www.ngltf.org/

ODT Inc. is a source of articles, tip sheets, reprints, materials, and training programs on cultural diversity. They feature a resource collection of books, audio tapes, articles, pamphlets, catalogs, and maps. 1-800-736-1293

SIETAR International (The International Society for Education, Training, and Research) is a professional organization of intercultural educators, trainers, and students with many chapters in the United States and abroad. http://www.sietarinternational.org/

Castle Consultants International cooperates with George Simons International to provide training in communicating and negotiating across cultures in Europe. http://www.castles.co.uk/

Newsletters

http://www.diversityinc.com/ is a source of news on diversity initiatives and has an online bookstore selling a wide a range of publications on diversity.

Managing Diversity Newsletter is a monthly publication in which some of the nation's top diversity experts offer ideas and practical suggestions about how to effectively manage the multicultural workforce. http://www.jalmc.org/mg-diver.htm

Resources available from www.diversophy.com.

Simons, George F., ed. *Eurodiversity: A Guide to Managing Difference for Value Within and Beyond the E.U.* Woburn, MA: Butterworth-Heinemann, 2002.

Simons, George F. and Dr. Bob Abramms, *Cultural Diversity Sourcebook.* Amherst, MA: HRD Press, 1996.

Simons, George F., and Dr. Bob Abramms, *Cultural Diversity Supplement #1.* 1996

Simons, George F. and Bob Abramms, eds. *The Questions of Diversity: Assessment Tools for Organizations & Individuals, Fifth Edition.* Amherst, MA: HRD Press, 1994.

Simons, George F., Dr. Bob Abramms, and L. Ann Hopkins with Diane Johnson, *Cultural Diversity Fieldbook.* 1996

Simons, George F. and Walt Hopkins. *Not My Type: Valuing Diversity.* A half-day, video-based training program for individuals and groups that encourages managers to question their misleading assumptions about other people and nurture the potential found in diversity. London: Video Arts, 2002.

Simons, George F., Selma Myers and Jonamay Lambert, eds. *Global Competence: 50 Exercises for Succeeding in International Business.* Amherst, MA: HRD Press, 2000.

Simons, George F., Carmen Vazquez and Philip R. Harris. *Transcultural Leadership: Empowering the Diverse Workforce.* Woburn, MA: Butterworth-Heinemann, 1993.

Simons, George F. and Amy J. Zuckerman. *Sexual Orientation in the Workplace.* Thousand Oaks, CA: Sage Publications, 1994.

Also, over 20 DIVERSOPHY ® classroom diversity and intercultural training games and online cusomized games.

Additional Reading

Bonet, Diana. *The Business of Listening*. Menlo Park, CA: Crisp Publications, 2001.

Dickson, Mary B. *Americans with Disabilities Act*. Menlo Park, CA: Crisp Publications, 1995.

Farrell, Warren. *The Myth of Male Power*. NY: Simon & Schuster Publishing Co., 1993.

Kaiser, Ward and Denis Wood. *Seeing Through Maps*. Amherst, MA: ODT, Inc., 2001. The Peterson Project maps are available at http://www.diversophy.com/maps.htm.

Kochman, Thomas. *Black and White Styles in Conflict*. Chicago: University of Chicago Press, 1981. Available from ODT, Inc.

Paulson, Terry. *Making Humor Work*. Menlo Park, CA: Crisp Publications, 1989.

Pollar, Odette and Rafael Gonzalez. *Dynamics of Diversity*. Menlo Park, CA: Crisp Publications, 1994.

Risser, Rita. *Stay Out of Court: The Manager's Guide to Preventing Employee Lawsuits*. Englewood Cliffs, NJ: Prentice Hall, 1993.

Scott, Cynthia and Dennis T. Jaffe. *Managing Personal Change*. Menlo Park, CA: Crisp Publications, 1989.

Simons, George F. and Lavinia Weissman. *Men and Women: Partners at Work*. Menlo Park, CA: Crisp Publications, 1990.

Tingley, Judith. *GenderFlex: Ending the Workplace War Between the Sexes*. Phoenix, AZ: Performance Improvement Press, 1994. www.gendersell.com

Webb, Susan L. *Step Forward: Sexual Harassment in the Workplace*. NY: Mastermedia Ltd., 1991. The author also publishes The Webb Report, a monthly newsletter to keep businesses up-to-date on the problem of sexual harassment. www.shadesofgray.com/webbreport.htm

Wederspahn, Gary. *Intercultural Services: A Worldwide Buyer's Guide and Sourcebook*. Woburn, MA: Butterworth-Heinemann, 2000.

Working Together

CRISP WORLDWIDE DISTRIBUTION

English language books are distributed worldwide. Major international distributors include:

ASIA/PACIFIC

Australia/New Zealand: In Learning, PO Box 1051, Springwood QLD, Brisbane, Australia 4127   Tel: 61-7-3-841-2286, Facsimile: 61-7-3-841-1580
ATTN: Messrs. Richard/Robert Gordon

Malaysia, Philippines, Singapore: Epsys Pte Ltd., 540 Sims Ave #04-01, Sims Avenue Centre, 387603, Singapore   Tel: 65-747-1964, Facsimile: 65-747-0162 ATTN: Mr. Jack Chin

Hong Kong/Mainland China: Crisp Learning Solutions, 18/F Honest Motors Building 9-11 Leighton Rd., Causeway Bay, Hong Kong   Tel: 852-2915-7119, Facsimile: 852-2865-2815 ATTN: Ms. Grace Lee

Japan: Phoenix Associates, Believe Mita Bldg., 8th Floor 3-43-16 Shiba, Minato-ku, Tokyo 105-0014, Japan   Tel: 81-3-5427-6231, Facsimile: 81-3-5427-6232
ATTN: Mr. Peter Owans

CANADA

Crisp Learning Canada, 60 Briarwood Avenue, Mississauga, ON L5G 3N6 Canada
Tel: 905-274-5678, Facsimile: 905-278-2801
ATTN: Mr. Steve Connolly

EUROPEAN UNION

England: Flex Learning Media, Ltd., 9-15 Hitchin Street,
Baldock, Hertfordshire, SG7 6AL, England
Tel: 44-1-46-289-6000, Facsimile: 44-1-46-289-2417   ATTN: Mr. David Willetts

INDIA

Multi-Media HRD, Pvt. Ltd., National House, Floor 1
6 Tulloch Road, Appolo Bunder, Bombay, India 400-039
Tel: 91-22-204-2281, Facsimile: 91-22-283-6478
ATTN: Messrs. Ajay Aggarwal/ C.L. Aggarwal

SOUTH AMERICA

Mexico: Grupo Editorial Iberoamerica, Nebraska 199, Col. Napoles, 03810 Mexico, D.F.
Tel: 525-523-0994, Facsimile: 525-543-1173   ATTN: Señor Nicholas Grepe

SOUTH AFRICA

Bookstores: Alternative Books, PO Box 1345, Ferndale 2160, South Africa
Tel: 27-11-792-7730, Facsimile: 27-11-792-7787   ATTN: Mr. Vernon de Haas

Corporate: Learning Resources, P.O. Box 2806, Parklands, Johannesburg 2121, South Africa, Tel: 27-21-531-2923, Facsimile: 27-21-531-2944 ATTN: Mr. Ricky Robinson

MIDDLE EAST

Edutech Middle East, L.L.C., PO Box 52334, Dubai U.A.E.
Tel: 971-4-359-1222, Facsimile: 971-4-359-6500   ATTN: Mr. A.S.F. Karim